Judith.

December 1983

Jobs in
the Textile and
Clothing
Industries

JOBS IN THE TEXTILE AND CLOTHING INDUSTRIES

Judith Taylor

Kogan Page

First published in Great Britain in 1983 by
Kogan Page Limited
120 Pentonville Road, London N1 9JN

British Library Cataloguing in Publication Data
Taylor, Judith
Jobs in the textile and clothing industries.
1. Textile industry — Vocational guidance — Great Britain
I. Title
338.7'677'02341 HD9861

ISBN 0-85038-744-2
ISBN 0-85038-745-0 (Pbk)

Printed and bound in Great Britain by
The Camelot Press Ltd, Southampton

Contents

Introduction

The textile and clothing industries are discussed separately in this book but there are of course strong links between the two. The textile industry processes textiles from the raw material to the finished cloth. The clothing industry takes this cloth and makes it into dresses, coats, suits, and a range of other garments.

Although the textile and clothing industries are separate, the word textiles is used as a general term to include all fibres, yarns and other materials which are made into fabrics, and the products which are made from these fabrics. Textiles are vital to our comfort, and this is what makes the industry an exciting place to work in. While you read this book, you are probably sitting on a chair covered in a textile fabric, with your feet resting on a carpet. Clothes are textiles, as are curtains, towels, sheets, blankets, and many other ordinary household items. Textiles have many other less obvious uses too — baize for billiard-tables, tennis ball covers, tarpaulins, sails, ropes, string, felt and typewriter ribbons are just a few. And there are many more industrial uses which people outside those industries know nothing about.

Let us have a brief look at both industries by taking one item, say a woman's dress, to see how it is manufactured. The label on the dress says that it is made from a mixture of polyester and cotton.

This means that two different fibres have been used. Polyester is a synthetic fibre, made by a chemical process, and cotton comes from the cotton plant. The two fibres may have been spun together to make a blended yarn, then woven or knitted into cloth, or the yarn made from pure polyester may have been woven or knitted with the cotton at a later stage. The yarns may have been dyed and then woven into a pattern, or the woven fabric may have been dyed, or printed. The cloth could have been finished in a number of ways; the finishes most appropriate for a dress are crease and fire resistance.

Some fabrics are sold in lengths for home dress-making, while others are bought by clothing manufacturers to be made up. Clothing manu-facturers often specialise in a particular type of garment, so the fabric may well go to one which makes women's light clothing, as it is called. After the designer has worked out a design, a pattern is cut and a sample dress made, so that any problems can be sorted out before the dress goes on to the production line. In the factory the different pattern pieces are cut out of the material several layers at a time. The pieces are then sewn together by machinists. The dresses are pressed, checked for faults, packed, and sent off to the retailer to be sold in shops and stores and via mail order catalogues up and down the country.

That, very briefly, is how a dress is made. In the following pages I shall describe the processes in a little more detail, and look at some of the jobs that are available in the two industries.

Acknowledgements

My thanks to all the organisations and individuals who have helped me with the preparation of this book.

The illustrations are reproduced by kind permission of British Man-Made Fibres Federation (page 26), Clothing and Allied Products Industry Training Board (pages 66, 67), British Wool Textile Industry (pages 21, 35, 39, 48, 50), International Institute for Cotton (pages 29, 41), Irish Linen Guild (pages 30, 37), John Taylor (page 36).

Judith Taylor

Part 1

CHAPTER 1

The Textile Industry

People have always needed clothes and other textiles for warmth, protection, ceremonial or religious reasons. Until fairly recently, manufacture has mostly taken place in the home, for immediate domestic use.

In the days when communications were very difficult, the manufacture of the various products developed around the ports, or near the supply of raw material or natural resources necessary for the manufacturing process — coal and fast-flowing soft water, for example. The manufacture of clothes took place in the big towns where there was a ready market. Although these factors are no longer so important, the industries remain dominant in the areas where they originated.

You will find that most manufacturers specialise in a particular process or product. This is partly a result of the industrial revolution, but it has become more noticeable over recent years. It is the most efficient and economical way of working.

The industries are subject to fluctuations in trade. The main reason is of course the difficult economic times, which affect all our lives. However, the textile and clothing industries are also vulnerable to changes in fashion, and have to adapt very quickly to new trends. For example, the development of man-made fibres was a severe blow to the manufacturers of natural fibres, but now cotton, wool, linen and silk have become popular again. Another problem is that many textile products can be manufactured very cheaply abroad, and in order to compete, British manufacturers have to work harder to keep the quality of their goods up, and prices down. This means that they have to use the most economical means of production possible.

Textile fibres are classed into three main types according to their source: animal, vegetable, and man-made. Animal fibres include wool and silk, vegetable fibres include cotton and linen, and there is a whole range of man-made fibres. There are also several 'minor' fibres which have either animal or vegetable origins, such as mohair, cashmere, alpaca, angora, jute, hemp and sisal.

Wool

Primitive man used the skins of animals as clothing. Sheep have always been easily domesticated and their skins are particularly warm and comfortable to wear. Eventually people realised that it was more economical to cut the wool, or fleece, from the living sheep and make it into cloth. As the wool quickly grew again, several fleeces could be obtained from the same sheep.

The wool trade has been a vital part of Britain's economy since medieval times. A mechanical knitting frame was invented by William Lee in 1589, and modern textile mills use powerful machines which can produce vast quantities of knitted cloth.

Spinning and weaving were important home industries until the eighteenth century industrial revolution. Spinning was generally the work of women and children, while men did the weaving.

Towards the end of the eighteenth century new, powerful machines were invented, and the industry began to move into factories able to process large quantities of material.

Cotton

Pieces of cotton fabric dating back to 3000 BC were found by archaeologists in the ruins of the ancient city of Mohenjo-daro, in what is now Pakistan. The Indian sub-continent was the centre of the world cotton industry from about 1500 BC until the sixteenth century AD. Arab traders brought cotton cloth to Europe in the Middle Ages, and it was also found in America by Christopher Columbus at the end of the fifteenth century.

Unlike wool, the cotton industry depends on raw material imported from abroad as the cotton plant needs a warm sunny climate. Woven cotton goods arrived in this country from the East during the seventeenth and eighteenth centuries, but they were luxuries which only rich people could afford. However, demand grew, and cotton began to be manufactured here. At first it was on a small scale, most of the work being done by men and women in their own homes.

New machinery included the spinning jenny, Arkwright's water frame, and Crompton's mule. In the same year that Arkwright invented his water frame (1769), James Watt patented his steam engine, and steam gradually replaced water power. One of the most important inventions was the cotton gin, invented in 1793 by Eli Whitney in the southern United States. This machine separated cotton fibre from the seeds, meaning that larger quantities of cotton could be supplied to the textile manufacturers. This machinery had to be housed in factories, and people went to work in them intead of at home.

The Manchester-Liverpool canal, opened in 1761, gave Manchester a direct link with the sea. This, together with atmospheric humidity and readily available supplies of coal, iron and water, made Lancashire the centre of the cotton industry.

Linen

Linen was known and used by the ancient Egyptians nearly 7000 years ago. The Phoenicians introduced the cultivation of flax (from which linen is made) to other parts of the world during the pre-Christian era but it was not until the Middle Ages that it became known in France. Skilled French workers took their knowledge of linen manufacture to Ireland, where it has been made since at least the thirteenth century, but for three or four hundred years it was used on a very small scale.

Linen cloth-making was a supplement to farming, the farmers growing the flax while their wives, daughters and servant girls did the spinning. The men then wove and bleached the linen. It was intended for use at home, but any surplus was sold to the merchants who traded at country fairs. This early cloth was coarse, and could only be woven in narrow lengths. During the eighteenth century weaving looms were improved, and wider and better cloth could be woven. This led to wealthy farmers hiring weavers to work either on the farmers' premises or in their own homes (the 'putting-out' system).

Towards the end of the eighteenth century linen manufacture was becoming an important industry. Apart from mechanical improvements, this was also the result of skilled linen workers settling in

Ireland from Europe because of religious persecution. The process of industrialisation was speeded up by the introduction of cotton manufacture into Northern Ireland in the 1780s. This was a well organised industry which used the spinning and weaving machinery recently invented in England. Mills were built close to the supplies of raw material (which had to be imported) and were concentrated around Belfast Lough. Workers were attracted from working with linen to working with cotton, and for a time linen suffered from the competition.

The industry revived in the nineteenth century when in 1818 the wet spinning method was developed which meant that fine (rather than coarse) yarn could be produced by machine. The use of steam power led to the building of large mills, which attracted many women spinners out of their homes, and by 1850 power looms were in use. Linen followed the example of cotton and many mills were established in and around Belfast.

Man-Made Fibres

We usually divide man-made fibres into two types: regenerated or cellulosic, and synthetic.

Cellulosic fibres, which include rayons and acetates, were the first to be developed. In the second half of the nineteenth century the French silk industry was badly affected by a disease which killed off the silkworms, and scientists tried to find ways of making artificial silk. In 1889 the first factory for making rayon from wood fibres was opened. A few years later a new substance called viscose was discovered, and this was used to improve the quality of rayon. Courtaulds, who had been an important firm of silk weavers, became involved in the production of viscose rayon and opened a factory in Coventry in 1905.

Fully synthetic fibres are made from by-products of coal or petroleum. Nylon was the first to be developed from research into plastics and rubber, by the Du Pont Chemical Company in the United States during the 1930s. There are now very many different synthetic fibres available, each with special qualities of its own.

Silk

Silkworms were first reared in China about 2500 BC. During the third century AD, the Japanese learned the secrets of making silk, and from there knowledge passed to India, and eventually Turkey and Greece.

In the Middle Ages, Italy became a great centre of silk manufacture, and nearly every Italian city had a silk industry; Spain was also an important centre. The manufacture was established in France in 1480, and a century later Flemish weavers were invited to England to found an industry. Later, more refugees from religious persecution in Europe settled in England, bringing with them knowledge of silk manufacture. They established centres in Spitalfields in London, Norwich, Colchester, Macclesfield, and Coventry.

CHAPTER 2

Fibres to Yarns

Natural and man-made fibres go through many processes before being spun into yarn — the continuous strand of twisted fibre used in weaving and knitting.

Wool

Today, wool comes to be manufactured in Britain from many different countries, including Australia (where there are said to be nearly ten times as many sheep as people), New Zealand, South Africa, and Latin America.

Different breeds of sheep produce different qualities of wool. The very best wool comes from the young merino sheep. Some sheep produce wool for a specific use. Harris tweed is made from the wool of the Scottish blackface sheep, which contains long hollow hairs which do not easily break down or take dye, and give the tweed its characteristic 'hairy' appearance. Each fleece also contains different qualities of wool (eg, shoulder, legs).

The fleece is removed from the sheep in one piece by shearing. Hand or powered clippers are used, and a skilled person can shear a sheep in less than five minutes. Each sheep may be shorn once or twice a year.

After shearing, the worst of the dirt is removed. The fleeces are then packed into bales and sent to be sorted and classified by number. The higher the number, the better the quality in terms of fibre length, strength, softness, etc. Short fibres are used for woollen cloth manufacture and long ones for worsted. The wool is cleaned of dust and sand, and scoured or washed several times in soapy water or with detergent to remove dirt and grease. Carbonisation is another process by which straw, burrs and other vegetable matter are removed by the use of acid, heat and pressure from rollers.

After cleaning, the long fibres from which worsted cloth is to be made are separated from those intended for woollen cloth. At this stage the latter may be blended with other wools, or with fibres from other natural or man-made sources. It is sometimes dyed at this point, too. It is machine dried before being fed into a carding machine. Here the fibres are separated and straightened by wire-toothed rollers, producing a twistless rope about 7mm (⅓ inch) thick called a slubbing. The slubbing is then drawn out into a fine, even strand or 'roving'. This is the last stage before spinning.

Qualities and Uses

The natural crimp and wave of the fibres make wool warm, elastic and non-creasing although it is less strong than some other fibres. It is liable to shrink unless carefully washed, and also prone to insect attack, although it can be treated against this. It is possible to remanufacture wool and this is also used for the manufacture of woollen yarn.

Worsted

The name worsted comes from a village in Norfolk called Worstead. Skilled cloth-makers came to

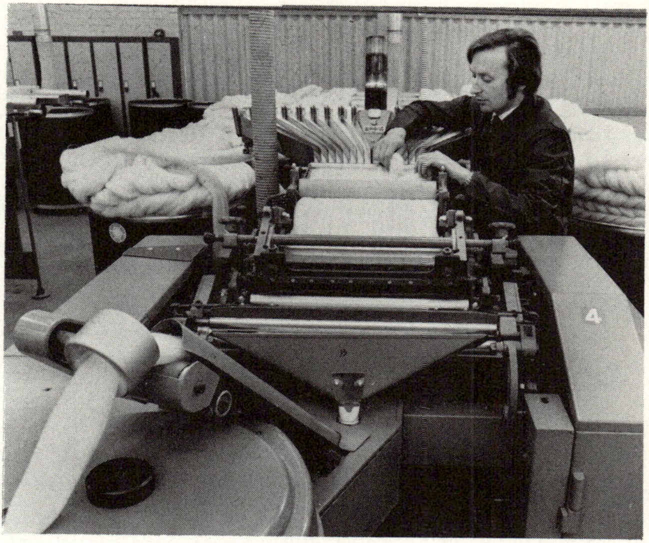

▲ Figure 1
Wool being combed

England from Europe in the Middle Ages to escape religious and political persecution, and introduced new methods of making cloth.

Worsted is made from new wool and the finished cloth is smoother and finer than woollen cloth. In order to achieve this, long fibres must be used, and the yarn must be smooth and round with the fibres running parallel. In woollen yarn the fibres cross and re-cross, giving a 'hairy' appearance.

There are many more processes in worsted manufacture, involving combing and gilling. These processes separate the long fibres (tops) from the short ones (noils), straighten the fibres and make them lie parallel (see Figure 1, above).

Cotton

The fluffy fibres surrounding the seeds of the cotton plant are the raw material from which cotton is made. These have to be ginned in a machine to separate the seeds from the fibres (the seeds are processed into food). The ginned cotton is then packed tightly into bales and either sent to a spinning mill in the country where it was grown, or exported.

When the raw cotton arrives at a 'cotton exchange' port (Liverpool is the main port in this country), samples are taken from the bales and classed according to their quality. There are three main types of fibre, varying according to where the cotton was grown:

- ☐ Long fine fibres from the West Indies, Egypt and the Sudan
- ☐ Standard fibres from the southern United States
- ☐ Short coarse fibres from China and India.

Most of the raw cotton imported into this country comes from Egypt and the USA.

The bales need to be 'broken' and the cotton cleaned. The tightly pressed cotton is loosened in a machine which also makes loose dirt, sand and vegetable matter fall out, and is then beaten in another machine to remove more impurities.

Cotton from different bales may be blended together. The fibres are then gathered into a fleecy lap, rather like cotton wool, and carded. The carding machine has a roller covered with small pins which comb and disentangle the fibres, and remove the short ones. The fibres are collected into a round sliver or soft rope, about 2.5 cm (1 inch) in diameter, and given a slight twist. High quality yarns are then combed, a similar process to carding, but more refined.

The next step is to combine several slivers into a strand which is drawn through rollers and eventually forms a sliver fine enough for spinning, which is called a roving. The roving is twisted slightly and wound on to a bobbin.

Qualities and Uses

Cotton is absorbent, strong when dry and even stronger when wet, and resistant to insects and high temperatures. However, it has little elasticity or 'stretch', is flammable, weak on exposure to sunlight and susceptible to mildew. A wide variety of fabrics are made from cotton, including chiffon, lawn, calico, denim, flannelette, drill, and corduroy. Cotton is very comfortable to wear, especially in hot weather. Blending with man-made fibres brings out the best qualities of each.

Linen

Linen fibre comes from the stem of the flax, a bushy blue-flowered plant which thrives in countries with a fairly cool, damp climate such as Russia, Germany, Belgium and Northern Ireland. The plants have to be pulled out of the ground, by hand or machine, because the lower part of the stem and the roots contain fibres.

The pulled plants are bound and stacked and left to dry, after which the seed heads are combed out. This is called de-seeding or rippling. The seeds are used to make linseed oil.

Retting is the next process. This causes the outer bark and inside core of the stalk to rot slightly, freeing the fibres. It may be done by leaving the stalks out in the fields, or by chemical treatment in retting tanks. When this process is complete, the stalks are washed and dried before breaking and scutching (beating) take place, in a mill. During these processes all woody matter is removed and the fibres are separated.

Hackling or combing follows. The bundles of fibres pass through a series of pins of increasing fineness. This separates the long fibres (line) from the short (tow), removes any impurities, and leaves the fibres lying fairly parallel. The long fibres are then drawn into a sliver of even, regular weight before being twisted slightly in the roving frame. This twist supports the fibres during the spinning process; the main twist comes later, in the spinning frame.

Qualities and Uses

Linen has similar qualities to cotton, but it is stronger and more absorbent. It creases badly, but modern technology can add crease resistance in the finishing stages of manufacture. It is cool and comfortable to wear, and its crisp, fresh look makes it popular for table linen. Its high absorbency means that it is suitable for towels.

Man-Made Fibres

As the name implies, cellulosic fibres are made from cellulose, which is found in wood pulp. The cellulose is boiled with chemicals to form a thick liquid. In order to make viscose rayon, it is then forced through fine holes in a nozzle (the whole thing is called a spinneret) into an acid bath, where the cellulose hardens into long continuous threads called filaments. The process is called extrusion. The filaments are then stretched and twisted to become strands of viscose rayon yarn. This is called wet stretch spinning.

Acetates and triacetates are also made from cellulose. The cellulose is treated with acid and water, then dissolved in acetone. The resulting thick liquid is spun directly into the air, and the acetate evaporates. This is called dry spinning. The filaments are then stretched and twisted into yarn.

In order to make polyamides and polyesters, a thick liquid is formed by heating chemicals which have been extracted from by-products of coal and petroleum. The chemicals are then forced into the air through the holes of a spinneret. This is called melt spinning.

The liquid for making acrylics and modacrylics is formed by dissolving the chemicals in a solution. It is then forced through a spinneret into the air (dry spinning) or into a liquid bath (wet spinning). The long filament strands are stretched and set by heating. Figure 2 on page 26 shows the different types of spinning.

Synthetic fibre filaments can be used separately as mono-filaments, or twisted together to form a multi-filament yarn. They can be crimped to give extra bulk or stretchability. If they are to be blended with other fibres they are cut into 'staple lengths' (similar in size to natural fibres), and spun like the natural fibres they most resemble.

Qualities and Uses

Synthetic fibres are in general stronger and harder wearing than natural fibres. They are also heat resistant, non-absorbent and rot-proof, usually quick drying and need little ironing. They tend to create static electricity but this can be reduced by treatment during manufacture, or by adding fabric conditioner to the rinse after washing. Yarns tend

Figure 2
Different methods of spinning man-made fibres

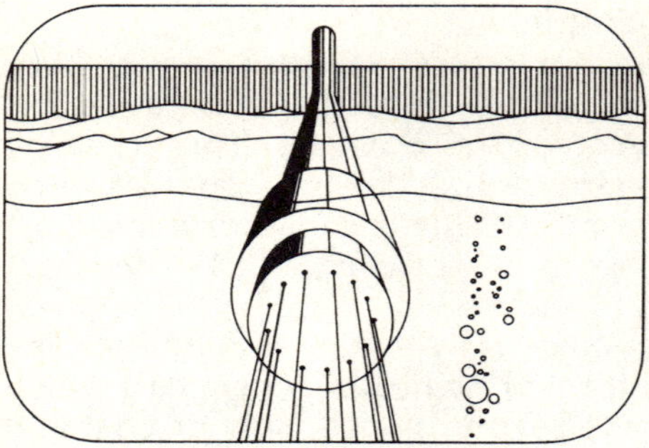

Wet Spinning
(Acrylic, Anidex, Rayon, Spandex)

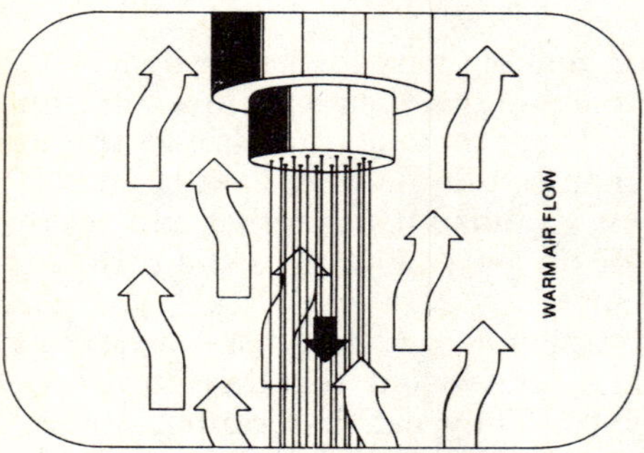

Dry Spinning
(Acetate, Acrylic, Modacrylic, Spandex, Triacetate, and Vinyon)

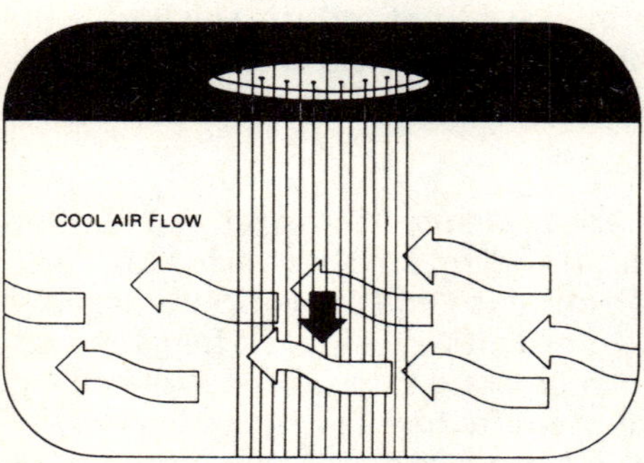

Melt Spinning
(Nylon, Olefin and Polyester)

to be shiny and slippery, and this can be offset by blending them with natural fibres. The resulting fabrics have the strength and easy care qualities of man-made fibres and the comfort and absorbency of natural fibres.

Rayon has properties similar to cotton but it has less strength when wet, which can cause it to stretch and lose its shape. It also creases. It has a silk-like lustre which makes it an attractive dress material. Acetates and triacetates are similar but the filaments are more elastic and have greater wet strength.

There are now a great many fibres, each suitable for a different use. Nylon, for example, which is very strong and recovers quickly after being stretched, is particularly suitable for underwear and hosiery. (Stockings are usually stretched over hot moulds in a special shaping machine.) Polyester is often used for net curtains, triacetate for permanently pleated garments, elastane for corsetry and swimwear, and orlon for knitwear. Because of their strength, man-made fibres have industrial uses too.

Silk

Silk comes from the cocoon of the silkworm, which is the larva, or caterpillar, of a large moth. A fluid and a gum are squirted through small holes on the caterpillar's head, called spinnerets, which together form a silk thread. The worm spins the thread around itself for two or three days until it is completely enclosed.

In its natural state the worm will change into a moth inside the cocoon, but on silk farms, where most of our silk is produced, the chrysalis is killed.

The cocoon is then softened by boiling water, so that the filaments of silk are separated from the surrounding gum.

Several cocoons are then unwound, reeled together, and 'thrown' or twisted to form a yarn. The yarn is wound into a skein or hank, and sent to the factory for making into silk fabrics. Waste silk from the cocoon is broken down into fibres and spun, either like cotton or worsted, depending on the length of the fibres. It is known as spun silk.

Qualities and Uses

Silk is strong, elastic and lustrous, and takes dyes easily. Although it can be weighted artificially, fabrics made from silk are often fine and light, and very beautiful. It is said that a sari made from silk, 18 feet in length, can be passed through a wedding ring.

Spinning

The purpose of spinning is to twist the fibres together so that they bind and are firm. When this happens they form a yarn. The fibres must be spun together evenly, and the yarn should be strong enough to withstand the strain put on it during weaving, knitting, and wear. Modern industrial spinning machines are fast and efficient, and can produce many thousands of metres of yarn per hour. There are several types of machine in use according to the yarn being produced (Figure 3, opposite).

Linen is often wet spun. The roving is passed through a trough of hot water which softens it

Figure 3 ▶
Rotor spinning of cotton; replacing the spindle

enough to be drawn out finely, before being spun on to bobbins (Figure 4, page 30). Some coarser yarns are spun dry. Yarns of varying strengths can be produced — strong for shoe linen, medium for table linen, and delicate for handkerchiefs.

Silk and man-made fibre filaments do not need to be spun, as such. Silk is twisted into yarn by 'throwing', and man-made fibres are drawn and twisted into yarn as soon as the filaments are made.

Fibres usually leave the spinning machine as a single yarn and for ordinary weaving purposes some remain this way. However, in order to strengthen or thicken a yarn two or more may be twisted or folded together, resulting in two, three or four ply yarns. Different yarns require different amounts of twist. Generally, the higher the twist the finer and harder the yarn will be. Cotton often has a very high twist, while wool has much less. Warp yarns, which need to be smooth and strong, have a medium to high twist, while weft yarns have a lower one. The twist can be clockwise, like the letter S, or anti-clockwise, like the letter Z.

◀ **Figure 4**
Wet spinning linen yarn

CHAPTER 3

Yarns to Fabrics

Yarns are made into cloth by various means including weaving and knitting; they are also dyed and may be printed, before finishing processes are applied.

Weaving

Weaving is the process by which yarn is threaded under and over other yarns at right angles to make cloth. Darning is a kind of weaving.

Nowadays the spun yarn must be carefully prepared before weaving can take place. The warp yarns (which run lengthwise) are wound side by side on to a beam at the back of the loom. This process is called warping. The yarns are then drawn forward through holes in upright wires called healds, which are fixed in a rectangular frame. There is one heald for each warp thread. The yarns pass through a heavy comb or 'reed' and are attached to a roller at the front of the loom. The finished cloth is later wound on to this roller.

If a new warp is identical to its predecessor in the loom, drawing in is unnecessary. Instead, the end of the new warp is tied or twisted to the end of the old one. This is called twisting in.

Meanwhile, the weft yarn (which runs across

the warp) is wound on to a bobbin or pirn, which fits inside a shuttle. If shuttleless looms are used, it is wound on to a special cone. The yarn is now ready for weaving.

The basic principles of weaving are what they have always been, despite mechanisation. The loom is a frame which holds one set of threads, the warps, running towards you while another thread, the weft, runs under and over at right angles. The weft thread is traditionally wound on to a bobbin or spool, and carried by a shuttle. The shuttles are housed in a shuttle box at the side of the reed, and are automatically released one at a time as required. They are knocked by a 'picking stick' through the warp threads. There are some looms which do not have shuttles at all. Instead, jets of water or air 'throw' the thread across the loom.

Before the weft can pass along, alternate warp threads must be raised by the healds to form a tunnel or 'shed'. The first line of weave, caused by the weft passing through the warp threads, is called the 'pick'. For the next line the raised warps are lowered and the alternate ones raised, making another shed. The reed keeps the threads evenly spaced and pushes each pick down hard against the previous one. These operations are automatic on modern power looms, and one weaver can look after several machines.

Types of Weave

The closeness of the weave can vary. For example, in cotton weaving, gingham may have 60 warps and 50 wefts per inch, and gauze 28 warps and 24 wefts. Generally, a closely woven fabric keeps its shape better.

Many fabrics have a pattern, either of colour or weave, or both (Figure 5, page 35). This is determined by the designer and translated into symbols for the weaver. The designs are drawn on 'point paper' on which squares are filled in to show how the warp and weft threads are to be woven. If the design is a new one, a sample or pattern may be woven by the pattern weaver for showing to customers.

The diagrams show how different weaves can be achieved (Figure 6, page 36). The first is a plain weave, for which alternate warp threads are raised for each pick. The second, hop sack, is similar, but warps and wefts are doubled. There are many other possible variations.

Elaborate and multicoloured fabrics are woven on Jacquard looms, where each warp thread is controlled separately (Figure 7, page 37).

Other Methods of Making Cloth

Knitting

Anyone who has knitted by hand will understand the principles of large-scale machine knitting. Instead of weaving yarns in and out of each other, like darning, knitting is a process in which rows of loops are interlaced to form a fabric. The old loop is cast off as the new one is pulled through. The loops are carried on needles, and there may be several hundred on a modern machine.

There are two types of knitting, both of which may be done on either circular or flat bed machines. In *warp knitting* the chains of loops run up and down the length of the fabric. Each needle carries one or more yarns and moves upwards in zigzag

Figure 5 ▶
A fully automatic rapier weaving loom capable of producing woollen and worsted fabrics

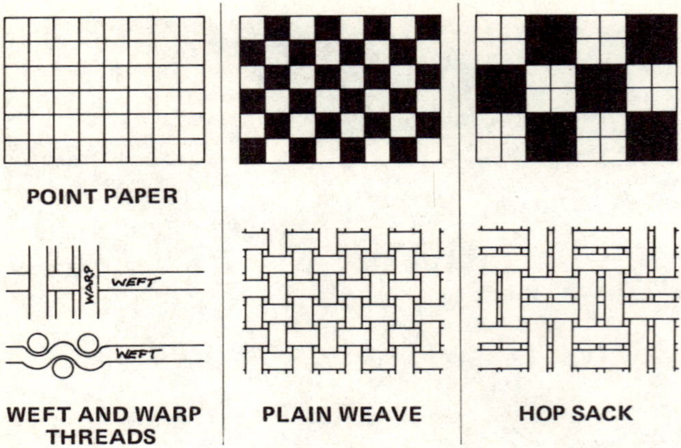

Figure 6 ▲
Weaving designs

movements. In *weft knitting* the loops run across the width of the fabric. A single yarn runs backwards and forwards across the needles, or round and round to make a tubular fabric if the machine is circular. Modern machines are capable of doing complicated stitches to produce a variety of fabrics.

Lace Making

Lace is made by twisting threads, usually of silk, cotton or linen, round each other to form an open mesh pattern. Lace making by hand is a very skilled craft, but most commercial lace is now made on a raschel warp knitting machine.

Figure 7 ▶
A linen damask tablecloth being woven on a Jacquard loom

Felt

Short wool fibres are used to make felt. They are mangled, steamed and compressed into a flat sheet. Felt is used for piano hammers, hats, carpet underlays, etc.

Bonded Fibre Fabrics

Fibres are sometimes bonded into a sheet. Adhesive may be used, or binder fibres which bond together when heated. Bonded fibre fabrics are used as interlinings and as backings for leather and plastics.

Laminated or Foam Backed Fabrics

These are made by sandwiching a layer of synthetic foam between two layers of fabric, or by joining a layer of foam to the back of a fabric. Adhesive is used, or else the fabric is heated to melt the foam very slightly and cause it to stick to the other fabric.

Dyeing

Dyeing is a very specialised process. There are several different types of dye and methods of dyeing depending on the fibre or the end result required (Figure 8, page 39). The development of man-made fibres, which take dye less readily than natural fibres, requires techniques to be updated constantly. Plain fabric needs to be washed and sometimes bleached before it can be dyed. Cotton fabric is often mercerised by immersion in caustic

Figure 8 ▶
A modern dyehouse; services are fed from below the suspended floor on which the stainless steel vats stand.

12

soda and stretching. This increases its strength and gives a smooth, silky finish, and means that brighter, deeper colours can be obtained. Linen can also be mercerised.

Fibres, yarns or fabrics can be dyed. Wool is usually dyed as yarn, in hanks. It is weighed, and then the appropriate chemicals are put into a vat where they are heated to boiling point. The hanks are soaked in the boiling dye — the longer they soak, the deeper the colour. If a blend of colours is required for, say, a Shetland yarn, then dyeing will be carried out after cleaning and scouring but before carding and spinning. Batches of different coloured fibres are put into hoppers to be mixed according to a 'recipe' devised by the dyer or colour matcher. The fibres are blended and carded to produce the right shade. Fancy fibres produced for the home knitting market require highly specialised dyeing and finishing techniques.

Cotton may be dyed at any stage in its manufacture, but linen is normally dyed as cloth. Dyes are often added to the solution from which man-made fibres are made.

Printing

Fabrics can be printed as an alternative to dyeing plain colours, or weaving or knitting yarns of different colours. Several methods are used, such as screen or transfer printing, and very often one company specialises in a particular method (Figure 9, opposite).

Figure 9 ▶
Roller printing of cotton cloth

Finishes

A wide variety of finishes may be applied to different fabrics. All fabrics need to be examined as they leave the loom, and any faults put right. *Milling* is a process used on tweeds and other fabrics which require a 'dense' texture. It felts the yarns together and shrinks the fabric so that the garment made from the cloth will not shrink or stretch in general wear. Woollens may be *brushed* and *steamed* to improve their surface appearance. The loose fibres on the surface of a cloth are sometimes *raised* to make it softer and fuller and subdue the effects of colour and weave. Worsted fabrics are *sheared* to remove surface fibres and give them a smooth, crisp feel. *Singeing* is necessary for smooth shiny fabrics as it removes all loose fibres and fluff from the surface of the cloth. *Tentering* or *stentering* is a process of drying fabrics while ensuring that they retain their shape. The cloth is stretched slightly and held by clips or pins while it dries.

Other, more specialised, finishes include stretch properties, which can be added to most fabrics. Shrink resistance, anti-pilling (pilling is the name given to the small balls of fibre tufts which are loosely attached to the surface of a fabric), anti-static properties, crease and flame resistance, and waterproofing are among the other finishes which can be added.

CHAPTER 4

Jobs in the Textile Industry

There are very many different jobs in the textile industry and it is not possible to look at each one individually in this book. You will also find that the same job is called by different names in different sectors of the industry, and areas of the country.

General

If you work in a production department you will find that some of the machinery is noisy. Most people get used to it very quickly. In some departments it is necessary to keep the atmosphere warm and moist. Again, most people quickly get used to this, but if you suffer from bronchitis or asthma, it would not be good for you to work in such an environment. Hygiene and safety are taken very seriously by both management and unions, and factories should be clean and light and well ventilated. Companies vary in what they provide for their staff. Most provide overalls and any necessary safety clothing and equipment. Larger companies have a canteen, staff shop, and recreational facilities, and some provide special transport to the factory.

The daily working period is normally eight hours, but may be operated on a shift system.

This means that the eight hours may be worked from 6 am, from 2 pm, or overnight from 10 pm (after the age of 18). There are usually rest periods every couple of hours or so. Overtime working is common, and part-time work is possible in many areas. Wages are negotiated between the trade unions and the employers' associations, and 'take home pay' is usually comparable to any other industry in the same locality. Examples of minimum rates of pay are given in Chapter 9.

Some of the work is heavy (ie, loading and unloading finished cloth and bales of raw material) but machine work does not normally require physical strength. However, you must be reasonably fit and agile, with good eyesight (with or without glasses), and in many jobs you must be prepared to stand for most of the day. Very good colour vision is necessary in certain sections of the industry, especially weaving, dyeing and printing. You should be tidy in your work, as untidiness, such as pieces of equipment or materials lying about, can be a safety hazard.

Craft/Operative Jobs

There are many occupations at this level, although it must be said that craft skills are less important than they were. Most involve running the plant and machines in the manufacturing process, but others are in cutting, packing, warehousing, inspection, mending and sewing. (There are also jobs in the canteens and offices, and as drivers and mechanics, but these fall outside the scope of this book.)

The job of a machine operative is becoming more skilled as machines become more complex, and you may have to look after a number of machines working at high speed. Your main tasks would be to check that everything is running smoothly and that the machine is supplied with the appropriate material and emptied, if necessary, when the process is complete. You might also be required to mend any broken threads, fasten off loose ends, etc. You would probably also be responsible for oiling and cleaning the machine, where necessary, and keeping the surrounding area free from dirt and loose material which could affect the quality of the product and also be a safety hazard. You need nimble fingers, quickness, and neatness. You also need to be alert and reliable, as a fault which is allowed to pass, or anything which causes a machine to slow down or stop, can upset the whole production of the factory and disrupt the work of several other people.

Specific skills vary from job to job, and training ranges from two weeks to several months. This will usually take place in the company, where you will be taught your job by an experienced instructor. You may also be given the opportunity to learn more about your job with a group of trainees at your local college. Generally, for this type of work, academic qualifications are not looked for but you should show a willingness to learn. However, if your job training involves attendance at a college, you may need to have CSEs at grade 3 or above, usually in mathematics, English and a science.

Spinning

Card attendants are skilled workers, as are the strippers and grinders who are responsible for setting and maintaining the carding machinery, and the fettlers, who clean the rollers. In cotton, the blowing room attendant has a skilled job, while the card, comb and draw-frame tenters, and the drafters, are semi-skilled. Ring spinners are responsible for the smooth running of their machines, for 'piecing' broken ends, and for cleaning and oiling the machines. Mule spinners are still needed, although ring spinning has taken over in many places.

School leavers often start work as members of a 'doffing' team, which is responsible for replacing full bobbins, but others start as learner spinners with a few weeks' training. Winders and twisters are usually given a short training programme as this work is fairly simple.

Weaving

Weavers nowadays have to look after several sophisticated machines, and are usually given up to three months' training. Warpers also need thorough training, as do loomers, enterers and twisters, and the latter three occupations are often filled by people with technical skills and qualifications. Other jobs, including winding the yarn, sizing and drawing, are semi-skilled.

Bleaching, Dyeing, Printing and Finishing

People are employed at all levels. Operatives are needed to fill and empty machines (heavy weights are lifted by cranes) and make sure that they are working properly. The printer is a skilled craftsman, who is in charge of the machine part of the printing process and responsible for the accuracy of the printed pattern as it appears on the fabric.

This means that he must set the printing machine and ensure that each part works correctly, maintain the supply of dye, paste or other printing medium, check the printed fabric, and make adjustments to the machine to rectify any faults. Thorough training is necessary, which is likely to include attendance at college. He needs to have good colour sense and eyesight.

Examining a woven fabric for faults involves a high level of skills, and therefore requires considerable training. The percher or taker in is responsible for detecting the faults in the first place. The piece of cloth is passed full width over rollers or bars suspended from the ceiling and carefully examined (Figure 10, page 48). Any fault which needs mending is marked with chalk. The burler takes out any thick places and draws knots to the back of the piece, and the mender sews in all threads of both warp and weft which have been left out or broken during weaving, and repairs holes and bad places. This latter job requires good eyesight and colour sense, with a full understanding of weaves and designs (Figure 11, page 50).

Skill and experience in many of these jobs may give you the opportunity for promotion to overlooker or foreman.

Case Study

☐ *Carol* is a cone winder working in a woollen spinning mill.

I have to keep the machine fed, replace bobbins, and watch for breakages, that sort of thing. A robot takes the cones away when they are full.

I first came here after leaving school when I was 16. They gave me two weeks' training. I left to have my little boy and I've been back nearly two years. I do

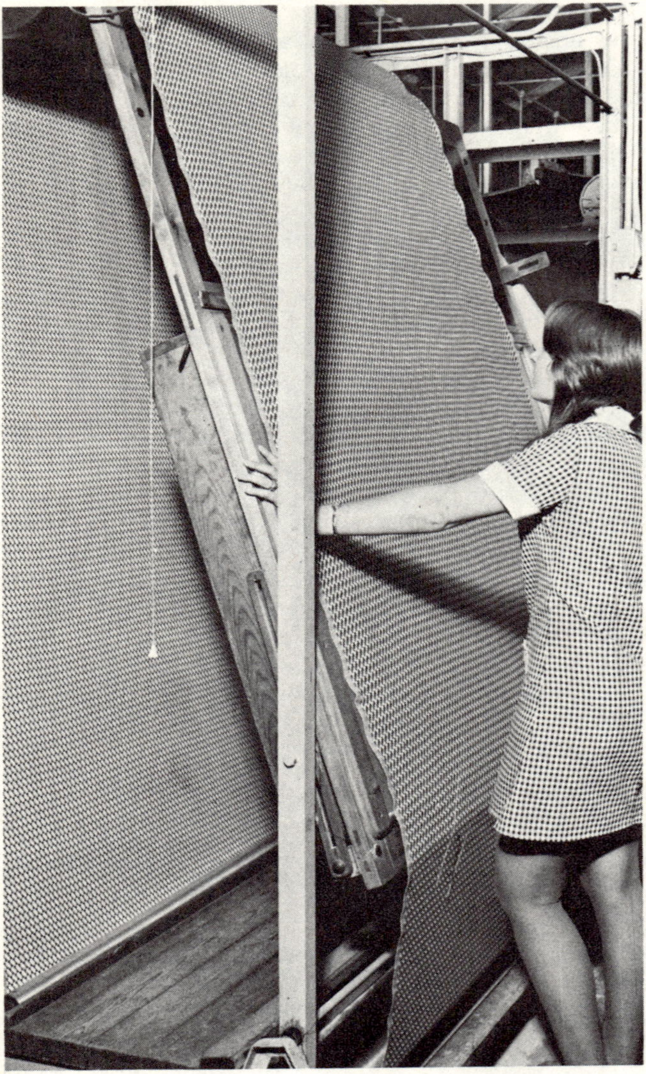

7.30 to 7.30 Saturdays and Sundays, so my husband can look after Andrew, and I'm at home during the week.

Technicians

Many different processes are now used to produce yarns and fabrics, and it is becoming more and more important that the people who keep the equipment in good running order have technical skills. Technicians are often key personnel in textile factories.

They are employed in production departments (setting, tuning, servicing and adjusting machines), in quality control laboratories, in design, in dyeing, printing and finishing. They need a combination of technical and mechanical skills, an interest in and knowledge of textiles, and as they may be required to supervise other workers, they should also work well with people. They should be competent in mathematics, a science and English language so that they can follow a course of further education, and many colleges now expect CSEs at grade 1 or GCE O levels in these subjects.

If we look at one or two technical jobs in more detail you will see the sort of skills that are needed. Technicians in dyeing, printing and finishing are responsible for ensuring that the fabric is treated to the right specification and standard. Their duties vary but can include some or all of the following:

☐ Working out the recipes for the chemicals or colours to be used for different fabrics and customer requirements

◀ Figure 10
Examining cloth at a Yorkshire worsted mill before final processing

- ☐ Calculating the settings for the correct speed, temperature, pressure and timing in the machine process
- ☐ Supervising both the mixing of chemicals or dyes, and the machine operation
- ☐ Testing the quality of products during trial runs and calculating any necessary adjustments to recipes and machine settings
- ☐ Liaising with the maintenance staff to ensure that the machinery is kept in good running order
- ☐ Keeping accurate records of fabrics, customer requirements, recipes and processes, to achieve the treatment required
- ☐ Making laboratory tests to ensure that the treated fabric meets the required quality standards.

Quality control is the responsibility of supervisors and technicians in all departments, but many firms also have a separate quality control department. Here, chemical and other tests are carried out to check such things as colour, thickness and strength of yarn, the weave, etc. The work varies according to what you are testing, but you will certainly need science O levels if you want to work in quality control, and some firms require higher qualifications.

The area of responsibility of an assistant carding engineer in a woollen yarn spinning mill covers quality, production, maintenance, waste control, labour control, communications, training, safety, and industrial relations. His tasks include checking each batch of yarn as it passes through his department, patrolling the department frequently to check that there are no malfunctions, making sure

◀ Figure 11
Repairing minor faults which have occurred during spinning or weaving. Illuminated screens are used to show them up.

that the engines are run at the recommended speeds and setting them up to meet specifications, recording on work sheets, delegating work, rectifying breakdowns, disposing of waste, making sure that safety measures are understood and adopted, and ensuring that all problems concerning industrial relations are dealt with promptly.

What the Job Involves

You will see from this that technicians' work often includes supervision. The wool textile industry now recognises a new grade of technician called a supervisory technician (although in practice the name of the job might be overlooker, carder, technical dyer, etc), who is responsible for the efficient operation of a department. This means processes and people. In order to do this work you will need a variety of skills, but you can build them up gradually. You must be practical and able to deal competently with machines and mechanical systems. You should be able to communicate clearly and concisely, both orally and in writing, so that you can advise and instruct those working under you and make reports about the working of your department. On a more personal level, you will need self-confidence, determination, and a willingness to take responsibility. You must not be colour blind.

Training

You will need a broadly based training because you will have to know all about the work of your department and understand how it relates to other departments. You enter the industry as a trainee or apprentice, and will be expected to have GCE O levels or CSE grade 1 passes in mathematics,

English and a science. Training will last four or five years, depending on your entry qualifications. You will be trained in the company you work for and on a day- or block-release basis at a college of further education. The college course is divided into two parts. At the end of three years, if you have worked satisfactorily, you will be awarded the Technician Education Council Certificate (or the Scottish equivalent). You could stop there, but if you want to become a supervisory technician you should go on to take the TEC Higher Certificate, which lasts another two years. In many colleges the Higher Certificate course includes training in supervisory skills (examined by the National Examinations Board in Business Studies, or NEBBS).

Alternatively, you could stay on at school to take A levels and go straight into the Higher Certificate course, although you may have to do additional units or even a bridging year to bring you in line with students who have followed the certificate course. You should check with your local college about entrance requirements before making firm plans.

If after taking the Higher Certificate you are keen to progress further, there are opportunities to study to become an Associate of the Textile Institute, or to do a degree (full time at the Scottish College of Textiles, Galashiels, or on a day-release or sandwich basis at Leicester and Huddersfield Polytechnics). This would give you the qualifications necessary to move into middle management.

Case Studies

☐ *Rashid* and *Graham* are studying for the Technician Education Council Higher Certificate in Textiles. They both work full time, with day release at college.

Rashid I left school and I used to go to the careers office now and again because I was looking for a computer job, but I suddenly changed my mind and thought I'd like to work in textiles. So when the careers officer said there was a vacancy in a firm a few yards away from my house I thought, Oh well, I'll take it. That was as an apprentice overlooker. So I went in for an interview, and I got the job. They were asking for two or three O levels — mathematics, English, and a science subject.

Graham At school the careers centre sent us for some interviews. I was offered two jobs at the time — one in engineering and one in textiles. I decided to choose textiles because at the time it seemed to offer more prospects and seemed a better job. Now I'm thinking of applying to Huddersfield Polytechnic, to go full time, to do a course in business studies. I can use my HTEC as entry requirements. If you went straight from school you'd need A levels. It's quite a high standard. I'm hoping to come back into textiles, on the marketing side or management.

Rashid This is our final year. We're doing HTEC and NEBBS. That's in supervisory studies. We've got exams coming up next month for NEBBS.

Graham I had two O levels and some CSEs. But the entry requirements for the TEC course, which is the first course, were CSE grade 3s in maths, English and a science subject. If you had an O level in maths or physics you could miss your science or your maths.

Rashid Which I did.

Graham That's only in the first year.

Rashid If you only have CSEs then they'll coach you up to O level standard. It takes three years to TEC and then two years to Higher TEC, plus the introduction of NEBBS. This is the first two years it's been introduced into part-time courses.

Graham It's one day and one evening a week. We have to work until half past seven at night.

Rashid It's better than it used to be. You used to come one day and then one evening on another day.

Graham I think having it all on one day makes it that much harder because it means you have more work to do at home. When you're working as well, it means you have to do college work at weekends. It's a broad course.

Rashid All processes are covered from raw wool to cloth. But then, whatever specialism you're working in, you'll be spending more time on that process.

Graham We all do practicals in our specialism, like I did combing and Rashid did spinning.

Rashid This last year we've had a project to do, right through the year. I started off with fibres of wool and terylene, blending them together and finding different proportions of blend and what qualities they were.

Graham Our TEC course has continuous assessment, which means that every six weeks you're having phase tests.

Rashid You have assignments every six weeks or so in NEBBS, that is to satisfy the TEC requirements, and then to satisfy NEBBS you sit an exam, plus a project.

Graham It trains you for a supervisory job.

Rashid The role of the supervisor has changed to some extent because at one time you were the boss of a department and knew everything about it — you did the repairs and everything — but now you're getting new electronic machinery where other people — specialists — have to come in and do the repairs. You don't like it because they're taking over some of your responsibilities.

Graham I think the computer age is just coming into textiles now and it's changing fairly quickly. A lot of the old ideas of machines have changed. I think it's becoming more and more important to have a qualification for a job because jobs are becoming more specialised.

□ *Trevor* and *Gary* are doing the same course.

Gary My mum got me the job. She'd been looking round for different jobs for me and she asked at work and there was a job available. I didn't know anything about it before I started. I just went. It's an apprenticeship and they told me I'd be doing a course.

Trevor When I first left school I wanted an apprenticeship. I started working for a firm of textile engineers — a labourer/fitter job — but they wouldn't give me an apprenticeship. So my dad — he works as a mechanic in a textile firm — he spoke to the manager of the department and said I wasn't satisfied where I was, and he said there was a vacancy for an apprentice technician. So I got the job through my father.

Gary We're in the second year of the HTEC. The TEC lasts three years, so that's five years altogether. We do lectures and practical work. They have all the machines here. We have exams every so often. There isn't a final exam. There is one for NEBBS, though.

Trevor Yes, there's one for NEBBS. I'm doing that. It's just part of the TEC course. You can take it if you want. It's all the same course but you have to take the exam to get the NEBBS qualification.

Gary I work in a testing lab, in a spinning mill. I'm training to be an overlooker but I'm doing testing now, testing the strength of yarns. Part of the training is that you have to work in different parts of the mill.

Trevor At the moment I'm working in the French combing department — that's using rectilinear combs. That's for worsteds.

Part 2

CHAPTER 5

The Clothing Industry

Before the invention of the sewing machine in the middle of the nineteenth century, all sewing was done by hand. Fashionable and everyday clothing, uniforms and domestic linens were hand made. Most of this work was done at home by women for themselves and their families, but there were tailors, dressmakers and seamstresses who sewed for the wealthy, while the aristocracy often employed people to live in and do necessary household sewing.

The invention of new textile machinery during the industrial revolution meant that there was a plentiful supply of cheap material, and in the nineteenth century ready-made clothes appeared for the first time. The demand for these clothes led scientists and engineers to look for a quicker and easier method of sewing, and in 1846 the sewing machine was invented. However, a good deal of sewing, especially of women's and children's clothes, continued to be done by hand until well into this century.

Nowadays only specialised sewing is done by hand. The modern industrial sewing machine is a powerful piece of equipment able to do a range of sewing jobs much faster than a domestic machine. Some are designed to do one specific job or stitch. Some can be programmed (like a computer) to do a certain pattern of stitches — useful for sewing labels or pockets. Other operations are mechanised, too. An electric band-knife is used for cutting through several thicknesses of material. The latest development is the use of computers at various stages of the manufacturing process although it will be some time before these are in common use.

General

The clothing industry is divided into three main sectors: wholesale manufacturing, which produces thousands of garments to sell to retail shops, stores, and mail order firms; *haute couture* or high fashion, which makes a number of original garments to show at the spring and autumn 'collections', and also makes garments to order for individual customers; and wholesale couture, which comes somewhere between the other two sectors. This sector makes 'model' garments in small quantities for sale through a limited number of retail shops.

Clothing manufacturers are often small, independent units which take orders from larger manufacturers or wholesalers. They are given the designs and the material, and they make up the garments. They are often family firms, employing a few extra workers. (The average manufacturer employs 41 people, which means of course that many are much smaller, and only 70 have more than 300 employees.) Some large manufacturers are entirely self-contained, with their own design, buying and making-up departments. Another type of firm designs the clothes and makes up samples, which are then sent to the larger manufacturers to be produced in quantity.

Firms usually specialise in a particular type of clothing. Sectors include:

Weatherproof outerwear
Men's and boys' tailored outerwear
Women's and girls' tailored outerwear
Overalls, men's shirts and underwear
Dresses, lingerie and infantwear
Hats, caps and millinery
Corsets and swimwear
Gloves
Other dress industries.

Dresses, lingerie and infantwear (sometimes called women's light clothing) is the largest group, employing a third of the total work force.

Working Conditions

The clothing industry, or 'rag trade' as it is often called, used to have a poor reputation. In the past, people had to work for low wages in poor conditions. Recently, however, things have greatly improved. A few 'sweatshops' still exist, especially in areas of high unemployment, but they are now the exception. Government regulations concerning health and safety at work, and the efforts of the industry itself, mean that the majority of factories are pleasant places to work in.

This is one industry where it is still possible to work your way up without formal educational qualifications. You may be trained in-company, or by going on a day-release college course, but basically you learn and improve your skills by doing the job. With time and experience you could become a supervisor, or even a manager, if you have the right personality and ability.

The majority of the work force are machinists, and they are usually trained in-company, although there are college-based courses which they could follow. The normal pattern is that an applicant for a job (usually a girl, as most machinists are women) is interviewed and given a trainability test. This is a fairly simple piece of sewing, like making a pocket, given to test whether she has the aptitude for the job. If so, she will be taken on as a trainee for about 12 weeks. At the end of that time she will be told (or will decide for herself) if she is suitable. If she is, she will be capable of doing fairly simple tasks on the production line. After that it is a question of building up skills and speeds. Pay is usually at a trainee rate to start with, and then piece work rates. If later she wanted to become a supervisor, she could go on a two-week instructor course.

CHAPTER 6

Fabrics to Clothes

Many workers are involved in converting the fabrics into the garments which we buy in the shops.

The Complete Process

All garments have to be *designed*. The style and the type, colour and pattern of fabric have to be decided before manufacture can begin. Only exceptionally talented designers can work free-lance, or in haute couture. The majority are employed by wholesale manufacturers. If you work as a designer you will have to take a lot more into account than your personal taste. Your design will be affected by: current fashions (it must appeal to a large number of people); the fabrics available to you; the type of clothes your firm normally makes; the manufacturing process; and, very important, cost. Most clothing firms have to work to a tight budget. You may have to select and adapt other people's designs, rather than create your own. You will be kept busy producing designs for 'collections' or groups of new garments which usually appear twice a year in spring and autumn. Designers get their ideas for these designs in many ways: from television, magazines, haute couture, regular visits to fashion shows, and occasional travel.

Once you have the idea for a design the next step is to sketch it and perhaps do some working drawings, showing the details. A *sample* of the garment is usually made so that any problems can be sorted out before it goes into mass production. The sample pattern is made from the designer's sketches, by the designer or a pattern maker. It is usually drawn on card, and then cut out. Standard pattern pieces (known as blocks) are sometimes adapted for use with the new design. A sample cutter lays the pattern on the fabric, making as economic use of the fabric as possible, and cuts it out. The pieces of fabric go to the sample machinist who *makes through*, which means that she makes the whole garment. Several samples may be made to show to different buyers. The machinist and the cutter then discuss any problems of making up with the designer. The finished sample garment will probably be put on a dummy to make sure that it hangs properly. A *toile* is often used, too. It is a rough guide of the garment, made in a cheap material, before the sample is made in the proper fabric. When made up it is put on the dummy and any necessary alterations are made at that stage. Many firms also employ models.

Before the design is sent to the factory for mass production, it must first be *costed* — taking into account the cost of the material, the amount which will be needed for each garment, allowance for different sizes, and so on. The responsibility for costing varies from one firm to another, and very often a separate coster is employed.

The pattern then needs to be *graded* for different sizes. This is a more complicated matter than simply adding another inch round the edge! For example, adding another two inches to the bust of a dress will affect the hips, length, armholes, shoulders, and possibly the neck. Someone may be employed as a pattern grader, or the work may be done by the designer, or the pattern cutter.

In the factory, the first job is to make a *marker*. This is a piece of paper the same width as the cloth from which the pattern is to be cut. The different pattern pieces are arranged on it so as to waste as little cloth as possible, taking into account the nap, one-way designs, etc. The simplest way of doing this is to lay full-size pattern pieces on the marker and arrange them to give the best layout. However, this can be difficult when long markers are used, and the pattern pieces and markers can be scaled down in size to make them easier to handle. A few large firms now use computers to do this work.

The *cutter* arranges a roll of cloth, called a piece, in layers on a large table. At the same time he inspects it for faults. This is called *laying up* and it can be done by hand or machine. The marker is laid on top of the cloth, and the cloth is then ready to be cut. The whole thing is held together by clamps. The cutter may first use a hand-held electric knife to divide the lay into easily handled sections. The pattern pieces are then cut by a larger stationary cutter or band-knife. The cloth is moved towards the rotating blade of the knife. Cutting has to be accurate or there will be problems when the pieces of cloth are sewn together. The cutter must make sure that the pile of cloth stays straight or the bottom layers may move and be badly cut. *Die-cutting* is a more mechanised form of cutting, but as it is more wasteful of material it tends to be used for cutting linings and trimmings and cheaper material. Again, there are now computers which can do this work.

Bundling is the last job before machining. The piles of garment pieces have to be put into sets of complete garments. Sometimes the job includes marking the position of buttons and buttonholes to help the machinist, and numbering the pieces.

The sample machinist made through; that is, she made a complete garment. In mass production, *sectional making-up* or *piece work* is common. This means that each machinist does one job — straight seams or waistbands, buttonholes or collars — as most modern machines do one job only. Because they are so efficient the work sounds easy, but they operate at speed and the machinist must be able to use hands and feet quickly and accurately to guide the material through the machine (Figure 12, below). Machinists also need to be able to thread their machines, and clean out the fluff and thread which collect there. Some sewing, such as

Figure 12 ▼
Trainee machinist and instructor

▲ Figure 13
Garment pressing

hemming and attaching buttons and trimmings, is done by hand.

The garments are *pressed*, usually with a hand-held steam iron, while they are being assembled. This is called 'under-pressing' (Figure 13, above). Completed garments are 'top-pressed', using an automatic press or steam iron. Certain clothes are pressed in a special way. Blouses and shirts are sometimes hung over a hot air blower, and men's jackets are often pressed on special shaped supports.

Inspection takes place at various stages in the production of a garment, but the final inspection is very important as it is the last one before the garment leaves the factory to be sold to a customer.

The inspector cuts off any hanging threads, and makes sure that there are no faults. If suits are being made, the correct jacket and skirt or trousers are put together at this point.

Packing is the final job. The garments may be covered in plastic and left on hangers, or folded neatly into a box or bag. They are then sent out to shops and other customers.

So far we have looked at the sections of the clothing industry where most of the work is to be found. There are other, more specialised areas, and we will look at these briefly.

High Fashion

Comparatively few people are employed in *haute couture* as high fashion is known. Competition for the few jobs which do exist is very fierce, and you have to be exceptionally keen and talented, and probably very lucky, in order to find one. Garments are made individually, sometimes for a particular customer and sometimes for the 'collections' of exclusive designs, shown in spring and autumn. A lot of the sewing is done by hand, and as the materials used are expensive, the workmanship must be faultless. If you are absolutely determined to work in this area, you should not settle for a temporary job elsewhere in the clothing industry as it is almost impossible to move from mass production to haute couture.

Bespoke Tailoring

This is still an important part of the industry, where suits are made to order for individual customers. Most tailored garments are made for men, but some are for women. Bespoke tailors also make overcoats, uniforms and sportswear (such as riding clothes).

Traditionally, the work is divided between tailors and cutters, and in larger firms there may be sales staff and a fitter. The fitter meets the customer, measures him, and advises him about styles and fabrics. Measuring is a skilled job, and must allow for individual characteristics such as round shoulders. A draft pattern on card is usually made for new customers and used for reference each time a new suit is ordered.

The cutter lays the pattern pieces on the cloth, allowing for matching fabric designs, and shrinkage, wasting as little cloth as possible. The pattern is marked on to the cloth and cut out, usually with shears. It is then passed to the tailors for making up. (Linings, facings and interlinings also need to be cut out and sewn into the garment.) In some firms the cutter has full responsibility for the production of the garment, including supervision of the sewing, but this is not always the case.

Sewing a high class bespoke suit is a very skilled job. The longer seams may be sewn by machine, but most of the sewing is done by hand. Different stitches are used for different effects, for example shaping the lapel, and buttonholes. Tailors are trained to do all aspects of the work, but in practice each one often specialises in a particular item, such as trousers, waistcoats or jackets.

A hand-held steam iron called a goose is used to press each part of the garment as it is stitched. Several fittings are also needed before customer and tailor are satisfied that the garment is ready.

The amount of care and handwork which goes into making a bespoke suit means that the finished product is very expensive to buy. Some firms now offer mass produced made to measure suits. The measurements of the customer are taken in the shop and then sent to the factory for cutting. Sometimes standard patterns are used, adapted to the size of the customer, or else each suit is cut out individually. The pieces of material then go to the production department to be made up, on a factory basis, with each worker responsible for a particular job.

Hat Making

Making hats is an old craft. It is a smaller industry than it was years ago, when men and women wore hats whenever they went out. In recent years hats have mainly been worn by ladies on special occasions, such as weddings, but fashions change and hats now seem to be popular again among the young.

Firms are usually small, friendly places. They often look bright and lively because of the quantities of different materials and trimmings, such as ribbons, artificial fruit and flowers, which are scattered about.

There are several different ways of making hats. Sometimes they are made by sewing together cut pieces of cloth, in a similar way to a dress or a blouse, except that the pieces are much smaller, of course. They can also be made by *blocking*. Blockers usually work in pairs, stretching a 'hood' of felt or net on a metal or wooden hat shape, called a block. The hood is then steam-pressed to the shape of the block. A special sewing machine is used to finish blocked hats. There is more hand sewing in millinery than in other parts of the industry. Trimmings such as net or ribbon or artificial flowers are nearly always fixed by hand. Straw hats are woven by hand or machine, and then shaped on a wooden block. Berets are knitted into oversized hats, and then felted and shrunk to the appropriate size, losing their knitted appearance in the process.

Glove Making

This is another specialised part of the clothing industry. It is also a very old craft. Many different materials are now used — leather, synthetics, knitted and woven cloth. If leather is used, it must first be stretched so that the finished glove will keep its shape. Each glove is then cut individually, using pattern pieces and a sharp knife. Cloth gloves are cut several at a time with a power-operated knife. Gloves can be sewn with an ordinary 'flat bed' machine, but there are machines which are specially designed for the work. Some experienced glove makers work from home but generally the work is carried out in a factory, which is usually a small and friendly place.

Theatrical Costumiers

This is interesting and varied work, but there is a great deal of competition for jobs. They make clothes for actors and actresses to wear on stage. Some large theatres have their own wardrobe departments, but others hire what they need from theatrical costumiers who employ their own dressmaking team.

The wardrobe department is often divided into production and maintenance. The production department designs and makes the costumes, and the maintenance department cleans and mends them when necessary. There are usually one or more designers, supervisors, and several dressmaking assistants. The job of the designer is skilled and specialised, and will have involved a full-time course at college. As a designer, you must work with the director, author, and the set designer, and decide together what is wanted, and you must be able to research period costumes, for example, to make sure that they are historically correct. And of course you need to be very talented.

The supervisor acts as a link between the designer and the wardrobe. She and her assistants interpret the designer's sketches and make the costumes. She buys the fabric and trimmings, or decides if existing costumes can be adapted, and usually has to work within a tight budget.

The dressmaking must be of a high standard to withstand the wear and tear of nightly performances. Illusions of richness can be created with cheap materials, and it is part of the costumier's skill to know when this can be done.

The television companies also employ dressmakers, but they will expect you to have had previous experience of theatrical costume work. The BBC, for example, requires you to have a City and Guilds or equivalent qualification in dressmaking, to be over 20, and to have had at least two years' experience.

Fitters and Menders

Some large department stores employ fitters and alteration hands. A customer may buy a dress or coat which needs shortening or altering in some way. You would need to talk to the customer and advise her about what might or might not be possible, and be capable of doing a variety of sewing jobs. You would start by working with an experienced hand, doing simple tasks, and then gradually take on more responsibility. Firms of dry cleaners also employ people to mend or alter clothes. Shortening or lengthening hems, altering waistbands, replacing zips and buttons and putting new collars on shirts are typical jobs which you might be asked to do.

CHAPTER 7

Jobs in the Clothing Industry

When you first join the clothing industry you will find that certain jobs such as cutting and bespoke tailoring are traditionally done by men, while others, such as machining, are considered to be women's jobs. There is no good reason why this should be so and you should not let this put you off applying for a job which is traditionally done by the opposite sex.

Designer

As well as having creative ability and being able to draw, you must also understand the technical side of the industry — how clothes are made, costed and marketed. You will need to have an interest in and awareness of fashion trends, a good colour sense, competence in pattern cutting and an understanding of costing techniques. You must be able to work as part of a team, with little or no direct supervision.

You are unlikely to find a job as a designer, especially in dress and millinery, unless you have taken a full-time course in design or fashion, and you would also be expected to have specialised in clothing design. Less qualified people with exceptional talent do occasionally manage to break into this field, but they are very few. Even if you are well qualified, you will probably be given further training in the techniques and production methods used by your firm.

Training

There are several ways to train as a designer. Degrees in Fashion/Textiles are offered by the Council for National Academic Awards at several colleges and polytechnics. They last for three years full time or four years on a sandwich basis. The entrance qualifications are high. You need at least five O levels and many colleges now require one or more A levels. English and two more 'academic' subjects should be included, and you should also show artistic ability. In addition, most colleges also require you to have completed a foundation year.

At the end of all this there can be no certainty that you will find a job as a designer, so you should be very sure that this is what you want to do before embarking on the long training. Further information can be obtained from the CNAA, 344-5 Gray's Inn Road, London WC1X 8BP.

DATEC diplomas and certificates in fashion are available in colleges throughout the country. They last two years full time and offer a good, practical route for 16+ students. Other colleges offer their own qualifications in fashion. Entry requirements are usually at least three O levels or the equivalent, and evidence of artistic ability.

You could begin your training by taking a three-year (full time) or four-year (sandwich) course leading to the examination of the Clothing and Footwear Institute. This will give you a complete training in clothing production, and you can study design as a main subject. This course is of a degree standard so you will need at least five GCE subjects, including mathematics and English, one of which should be at A level. Further information is available from the Clothing and Footwear Institute, Albert Road, London NW4 2JS.

The City and Guilds of London Institute courses in fashion (780) are run at several colleges throughout the country. They are usually available on a day-release or evening class basis. If you are already working in the clothing industry and have an ambition to move into design, or are simply interested in learning more about the subject, these courses might appeal to you.

Salaries vary greatly, and designers normally negotiate salaries and conditions of service on an individual basis.

Pattern Cutter/Grader

Pattern cutting and grading may be separate jobs, or combined. The work involves interpreting the designer's drawings into the form of a paper or card pattern, cutting this out, and then grading it for different sizes. You should have good eyesight, with or without glasses, steady hands, a good understanding of the process of making clothes, and mathematical ability. The latter is particularly important if you are to grade patterns.

Training

There are several part-time courses available, varying in length from a few weeks to one year. Your employer might arrange for you to attend your local college on a day-release basis. Some colleges also offer evening classes. Alternatively, you could do a broader based training with a specialisation in pattern cutting/grading (TEC or CGLI 460).

Sample Cutter

The sample cutter cuts out individual garment pieces with shears, making careful use of the fabric. She marks sewing lines and instructions on to the cloth with chalk. The pieces then go to the sample machinist for making up into sample garments. Training is usually a combination of on the job training with a part-time college course.

Cutter

Accuracy is very important, as are good eyesight (with or without glasses) and a steady hand. You will also need to show some academic ability. Most employers now expect you to have two or three GCE O levels or CSEs at grade 1, including mathematics. This subject is important because of the need to use garment sizing tables and plan the use of cloth. The ability to distinguish between colours, weaves, and types of cloth is also important. You must be prepared to spend most of the day standing.

Cutting has always been seen as one of the key jobs in the clothing industry, and once you are qualified there are good opportunities for progression. When you are first taken on by a firm you will be given simple tasks to do, under the supervision of an experienced cutter. You will gradually be given more skilled and responsible work until you are fully trained. You could then move on to more skilled and possibly supervisory roles — cutting room foreman or manager. Cutters sometimes also move into pattern cutting and grading.

Training

Training is both on and off the job, and might involve four years in all. You will be expected to take City and Guilds examinations during this time. You will probably follow course 460 — Clothing Craft — with a special option in wholesale cutting. It is normally taken as a day-release course although it is possible to study full time in some colleges. (For further details about this course see page 110). Alternatively you might study for the TEC/SCOTEC diploma or certificate in clothing.

Machinist

Machining is probably the job most people have in mind when they think about working in the clothing industry, but by now you will have realised that it is only part of the garment-making process. However, it is a large and important part, particularly in terms of people employed. Conditions vary, but most machinists work with several others in a large room. This means that your surroundings will be busy, usually rather noisy, and you will have to learn to ignore distractions and concentrate on your work. You should be good with your hands and have good eyesight (with or without glasses).

A really skilled and experienced machinist may get the chance to work with the design team, making up sample garments. You need to have mastered all the machining skills so that you can make a complete garment without supervision.

If you get on well with other people, are able to organise work efficiently and like responsibility, you could become a supervisor or training instructor, and in the clothing industry it is always possible for the right people to move into even higher jobs.

Training

Training is generally carried out in-company. This may be in a group, with other trainees, or on the job, with an experienced operator. A typical training scheme involves a programme of exercises for machine control, followed by machine exercises for a particular job. You may also be given talks about the company you work for, the other processes which take place in the factory, and safety (this is very important when you work with fast and powerful machines). If you are keen to learn more about your job your employer might send you on a day-release course such as the new City and Guilds course 460, Clothing Craft. Some colleges offer this in the evenings.

Bundling, Stockroom Work, Pressing, Quality Examination, Packing and Despatch

For all these jobs you need to be careful, methodical and patient. Pressers must not mind standing for most of the day in a warm atmosphere.

Training

Training is on the job, under the supervision of an experienced worker. You could also attend day-release or evening classes. CGLI 460 (see page 110) would be the most suitable course because you would do common 'core' studies to give you an understanding of the industry as a whole, as well as more specialised studies of wholesale garment manufacture. You could stop after the first year, or go on for another one or two years.

Supervisor

I have said that it is possible to work your way up to becoming a supervisor from almost any of the jobs mentioned in this part of the book. You may like to know more about the work of a supervisor.

The supervisor's job is to organise the work of a section or department of a firm. This means making sure that enough garments are produced to satisfy the company's targets, that they are of good quality, and that the correct methods of production are used. You must ensure that the members of your team work well together, be able to settle minor disputes, and generally see that the work of your section goes smoothly. The supervision of training would also be your responsibility.

Experience of the industry and the right personality are more important than academic or great technical ability. You must know the work of your department well so that you can see whether the rest of the staff are doing their work properly. You need to have confidence in yourself, but also be tactful and patient. You should be given training in supervisory skills as there are several short courses available.

Bespoke Tailor and Cutter

Although academic qualifications are not essential, most employers now prefer to take on people with GCE O levels or CSEs at grade 1. Mathematics is particularly important. You need to be able to work as part of a team, with a minimum of supervision.

You must have a steady hand and be careful and accurate in your work. You should have good eyesight (with or without glasses), and a cutter must be able to spend a lot of the day standing. You may have to meet customers to find out what they want and advise them about materials and styles, so you should be able to talk to all kinds of people confidently but politely.

Training

As with other clothing crafts the best course for you will probably be CGLI 460 (page 110), which will give you a broadly based training with specialisation in handcraft tailoring or retail bespoke cutting. Alternatively you could take a TEC certificate or diploma in clothing. These courses can be taken full time (in which case they would be followed by a period of on the job training with your employer) or on a day- or block-release basis.

Hat Maker

You need to have good eyesight (with or without glasses) and steady hands if you want to be a cutter, and skilled fingers and a liking for fine work if you want to do hand sewing. Blockers need to be quite strong and not mind standing for most of the day in a warm steamy atmosphere. Designers should have up to the minute knowledge of fashion trends (both in millinery and elsewhere, as hats need to co-ordinate with coat and dress styles). You also need to understand the production side of fashion and be able to keep your designs within certain cost limits. Sometimes a skilled milliner with a flair for design can become a designer, but you would normally be expected to have had art school training. Other groups of staff are given on the job training.

Glove Maker

You need to be careful and accurate, with skilled fingers and good eyesight (with or without glasses). The work is small scale and requires great accuracy. Some jobs involve standing for a large part of the day.

Training

Training is generally on the job and given by a qualified, experienced person. The length of time it takes varies according to the job: a few weeks for simple machining, and up to three years for an apprentice leather cutter.

Theatrical Costumier

If you want to work in the theatre you must be adaptable, prepared to work unsocial hours, mature, and willing to accept a rather unstable life. If you are not sure whether you would like it or not, offer to help your local theatre or amateur dramatic group. This experience should help you to decide if you really want this kind of work.

You will need to use a wide range of skills, as you will be called upon to make costumes for men and women, historical and modern day, and maybe some rather unusual items — headgear for bishops and princes, wings for pantomime fairies, and even animal costumes (think of Dick Whittington and his cat!).

Training

Although you may be lucky and find an employer who will train you, you would be better advised to get some training before you start writing to theatres and applying for jobs. A qualification in dressmaking (the CGLI course in fashion, 780, includes dressmaking) would be a good start. Three colleges (Canterbury, Mabel Fletcher and Wimbledon) offer full-time courses in theatre wardrobe. Entry requirements are five GCE O levels or the equivalent, and evidence of artistic ability and sewing skills. The courses are all different, and last between one and four years. You must have both qualifications and experience before you can hope to get a job in television.

Salaries

Wages vary according to the size of the firm, the part of the country, and the level of responsibility involved in the job. Apprentices and trainees are paid a fixed wage which usually increases as they go through their training. Machinists, milliners and glove makers are usually paid piece rates. Bespoke tailors and cutters are also paid for each completed garment, and often earn a very good salary. Supervisors are usually paid a fixed wage, and possibly a bonus payment based on the output of their section. Some examples of minimum rates of payment for the year ending April 1982 are given in Part 3.

Case Studies

☐ *Carmela* is a sample machinist.

We don't do production work here, just samples. There's supposed to be one of each style but sometimes repeats

come round and we make them up as well.

We do everything relating to the dress after it has been cut. We have to use every machine: over-locker, buttonholer, super-locker — that does the edges of frills and suchlike where the over-locking shows. The over-locker locks seams together and things like that. The plain stitch machine does seams.

It's not difficult to use the different machines. If you are used to one machine and can thread it you can go from one to the other. It's like if a person can read, you are supposed to be able to read the *Mirror* or any such thing. It's the same.

We do finishing and pressing here too. The pressers use a kind of iron, but they call it a machine. It is a machine to the pressers. There's some hand work — buttons, press studs, hooks — lots of different bits and pieces.

The pieces for the dress come rolled up in a bundle with a sketch and instructions. The arrows show the cutter which way to lay the pattern. If she cuts it wrong then I get it wrong.

It takes about an hour or an hour and a half to make a dress. Some are more complicated — you need to join together lots of different bits and that takes time. Half-way through we put it on a dummy to see that it is coming up right.

We can use the machines at lunch time to do our own sewing. I make all my family's clothes.

I used to work at home making samples on my machine. They sent the material and pattern and I cut it out. Then I worked for a firm where I was the sole machinist, and there was just a pattern cutter and a designer. I did my own work and didn't have to ask anyone. I've been nearly two and a half years with this firm. I like to work in a small firm doing samples — you know everything that's going on.

□ *Christina* is a sample cutter working for the same firm.

The designer sketches a design. It goes to the pattern cutter and he interprets it on paper. Then the pattern comes to me and I cut it out and then it goes off to the machinist to be made up and if it is sold it goes into production. Sometimes the sample cutter does the costing but here we have a separate coster. She trained in textiles. You often find this — people who've been trained in one aspect of the trade change over. I don't know why she changed.

I have to cost in a way. When Mary comes to actually cost it to go into production, I've got to make sure that it's economical otherwise it's just wasting everybody's time — it's wasting her time and everybody else's. So if I think it's uneconomical the pattern then has to be altered. We do sizes up to 22 here so obviously the coster has to take that into account.

We rely on outworkers, that is people who work in small units or at home. This is the design and sample room, so we just do the first designs here, then if they're wanted they go to an outworker. We just do dresses and separates.

Part 3

CHAPTER 8

Finding a Job

When you started to read this book you may have thought, 'What's the point in choosing which job to do when I know I shall be lucky to get a job at all?' At the start of any discussion about jobs it must be said that they are not easy to find. You must be prepared to work at it and you must make sure that you go about your job search in the right way.

Thinking about Jobs

First of all you must plan ahead. You may not want to think about jobs when you are still at school and the world of work is a year or two off, but the sooner you start the better prepared you will be when the time comes to job-hunt in earnest.

Begin by thinking about yourself, and about the type of work you think you would be good at, and enjoy. Would you like to work outdoors or indoors? With machines, with people, or doing office work? Do you like being in a noisy, lively environment, or do you prefer a quieter existence? Are you good with your hands, with figures, with people? Are you interested enough in academic subjects to consider studying for a qualification which will help you to get a better job? What do you want from a job? Money, of course, but you may find that a job which seems poorly paid at first pays much better later on when you are trained. Do you want an interesting, and perhaps demanding, job, or a routine one? Do you like responsibility? Is making new friends important to you? You will need to think about all these things.

What you decide will of course be affected by where you live. Unless you are prepared to move away from home your choice will be limited by the industries and commercial businesses in your area. It's best to avoid a long journey to work, especially in your first job.

You may need the advice and help of experts. Find out what your school has to offer first of all. There may be a teacher who is responsible for careers, or you could talk to your class teacher. Does your school have a careers library? If not your local library should have a section containing books and pamphlets about jobs. Ask the librarian to point it out to you. You don't have to be a member of the library in order to look at the books there.

Every local authority runs a careers service, and there is an office in all towns of reasonable size. It will be listed in the telephone directory under the name of your local council. You can go there any time, but the careers advisers also go out to visit schools, usually during the winter term, to talk to 5th and 6th formers about job prospects, and to interview pupils individually. The adviser will help you to decide what to do and how to set about doing it. An interview with the adviser gives you the opportunity to talk about yourself, and the work you want to do, to someone who knows about local job prospects. It also gives you the experience of being interviewed.

Representatives of local firms may come to school to give talks. They often know what their needs will be well in advance, and if you are interested you may have to apply some time before the end of the school year. This is particularly true if a firm is offering traditional craft apprenticeships.

You are likely to be given a lot of advice. The first piece is to be realistic about the work you want to do, and also adaptable, so that if your first choice proves impossible you can consider other ideas. Adaptability is very important. Modern life demands that we change our jobs and even our homes to keep up with shifting patterns of employment. Throughout your working life you will have to be ready to learn new techniques and manufacturing processes, and the quicker off the mark you are to learn these things, the better chance you will have to get and keep a good job. This applies to people in all kinds of work, and at all levels.

Following on from this is the need for qualifications and training generally. The development of new, advanced machinery, especially in the textile industry, means that the character of many jobs has changed. The old crafts are dying out, and the key person in many firms is the technician. Jobs generally are becoming more skilled, and there are fewer vacancies for unskilled machine operators.

In other words, you should get whatever qualifications lie within your capabilities. You don't have to stay on at school to study. You can do a full-time course at a college of further education, or you could get a traineeship or apprenticeship with a local firm who will arrange for you to do day or block release at the college. In a competitive world the person with two or three GCE O levels or CSEs, a City and Guilds or TEC qualification, has a better chance of getting a job than the person without any qualifications at all.

However, if academic skills are really not your strong point, don't despair. There are other ways of impressing an employer. An important one is to get some kind of work experience — in your chosen area if possible but anything is better than nothing. An employer will always be interested to see someone who has had some experience of working life, and it will give you something to talk about at an interview.

How do you get work experience? You might be able to find a Saturday or holiday job — even a paper round shows that you have the discipline to get up early to do the job. Some schools are able to arrange work experience for 5th and 6th form pupils. Ask your class or careers teacher if there is such a scheme. The work experience usually lasts one or two weeks, or one day a week for a few weeks. It will give you experience of working conditions, you may make useful contacts, and you should be able to ask the firm for a reference or testimonial later on.

Looking for Jobs

Let us say that you are nearing the end of your final year at school, and you have decided that the time has come to start looking for a job in earnest. It's a good idea to make a list of facts about yourself — your name, address, age, education, hobbies, etc. It will be useful to refer to when you are filling in application forms (they nearly always ask for the same information) and you can make copies to enclose with any letters you write to possible employers, and to hand over at interviews.

The Manpower Services Commission suggests that you call this list a Personal Information Chart,

PERSONAL INFORMATION CHART

Name ______________________ **Age** ____________

______________________ **Date of Birth**

Address ______________________ ____________

____

______________________ **Tel No** ____________

EXPERIENCE

☐ Jobs/Training

☐ School

☐ Interests/Achievement

EQUIPMENT I CAN USE

REFERENCES

or PIC, and it is shown on page 93. You will see that it is divided into sections, with headings. Under Jobs you should put down any work you have done, such as baby sitting, car washing, or Saturday jobs. Training should include special courses at school, or evening or Saturday classes. Put down the name of your school or schools with the years you attended, and any exams you have taken or are about to take. You could also add any subjects you particularly like, such as sports or woodworking. In the next section you should list anything you enjoy doing — riding your motorbike, watching television, sewing, cooking — anything which interests you. Think hard about the equipment you can use. Ordinary things like a telephone, calculator, or sewing machine could go in here, and of course if you can use more specialised equipment, this should certainly be listed.

Finally, references. These are what previous employers or family friends can give to a prospective new employer. You need to write down the names of two people who will answer a few questions about you by phone or in a letter. (Don't forget to ask them first if they are prepared to do this for you.) The employer wants to know if you are reliable and trustworthy, and whether you are fitted to do the job for which you have applied. You shouldn't ask relations to give you references, but old family friends, your doctor or teacher, would do very well.

The next thing to do is register at your local careers office. The people there will give you support and general advice, and they have up-to-date information about current vacancies and youth opportunity schemes. Registering will also make you eligible for supplementary benefit later on, if you fail to get a job. If you are disabled you may find that there is a specialist careers adviser to help you.

The careers office helps young people up to the age of 18. After that you become the responsibility of the Employment Office or Jobcentre (the address will be listed in the telephone directory under Manpower Services Commission). These offices have areas where current vacancies are displayed on cards; you can go in and look at any time. If you see a job that looks interesting, tell the receptionist, giving the reference number on the card. The receptionist will tell you more about the job and arrange an interview for you if it seems suitable. You should make regular visits to the Jobcentre as the jobs on the cards are changing all the time. You can make an appointment to see an employment adviser if you need more help and advice. If you are disabled, there will be a specialist Disablement Resettlement Officer to help you.

The Careers and Employment Offices do not know about every available job, so you must also look out for yourself. Read the situations vacant column in your local paper, and look out for notice boards outside large factories, in youth clubs, community centres and shops. Newsagents' windows are very good places to look. If you know the sort of job you want, try to get hold of some trade magazines (such as *The Draper's Record* for the clothing industry). Your local library should be able to help. Local radio stations often have a job spot when local vacancies are listed, so find out when this is and listen regularly. Talk to friends and relatives and ask them to let you know of any suitable jobs. And if you do see or hear of something — follow it up quickly. You won't be the only person who is interested and if you dither about for a week you may find that the job has gone.

An advertisement should tell you whether to telephone, write or call in person. If you telephone, have the advertisement in front of you and a diary, pencil and paper to hand. If you are in a pay phone make sure that you have enough coins with you to feed the machine. If someone's name is given in the advertisement, ask for that person; if not, for the personnel officer. Give your name clearly and say what job you are interested in.

If you write make sure that your name and address are clear and legible. Write a fairly short letter, stating which job you are interested in and why. Enclose a copy of your personal information chart, unless you are asked to complete an application form supplied by the employers.

The Interview

Once again you should plan ahead. Look up the address on a map and make sure that you know how to get there, and how long the journey will take. Allow for your bus to be late, and for getting lost! It could happen.

Try to do some homework before you go. Find out as much as you can about the firm and the work it does. If, for example, it is a cotton spinning firm then go to your library and borrow one or two books about cotton, or talk to people who already work for the industry. Any employer will be impressed by someone who shows an interest in the work of the firm.

Once there, you will probably be shown into an office where a receptionist or secretary will ask you to wait until the person who is to interview you is ready. First impressions are important, so look clean and tidy. While you are waiting have a look at your personal information chart to remind yourself of what you have said there. It's easy to forget things when you are nervous. Think up a few questions to ask the interviewer — you are sure to be asked if there is anything you want to know. An interview is, or should be, a two-way process; you need to find out about the firm as much as they want to find out about you.

When you are told to go in, knock on the door first (unless it is opened for you). Be prepared to shake hands with your interviewer. When told to sit down try to sit comfortably, and relax. Try not to fidget, and don't smoke unless the interviewer offers you one.

When talking, try to sound reasonably confident without overdoing it. Allow the interviewer to explain things to you, even if it's something you know already. Be prepared to tell the interviewer why you are interested in the job you are applying for. He or she will be impressed with someone who sounds bright and enthusiastic. When answering questions try not to say 'yes' or 'no', but enlarge a bit. For example, if you are asked whether you have any hobbies, tell the interviewer about them. When the time comes try to think up one or two questions to ask, even if you seem to have been told everything you want to know. (If you really can't think of anything, say something positive like, 'You seem to have covered everything'.) When you have finished asking your questions, say so. The interviewer will make it clear when the interview is over, and you should thank him or her for seeing you.

Apprenticeships and Traineeships

Apprenticeships tend to be linked with craft-based

jobs, and traineeships with technical jobs, but the terms are often interchangeable. Traditionally, an apprenticeship involved a binding agreement between parent or guardian and employer, which covered wages, service, conditions of work, study periods, programme of carefully chosen work and training, and procedures in case of dispute. The apprentice would agree to remain with the employer for a specific period of time — rarely less than three years — at the end of which, provided his study and work were satisfactory, he would be recognised as skilled at his craft. Work would usually be as assistant to a skilled employee, and there would be an agreed amount of on the job and off the job (college-based) training. Nowadays an employer might offer a traineeship, similar to an apprenticeship, but adapted to modern needs. All the details should be explained at an interview, and if you are asked to sign a contract you should read it carefully to find out what your and your employer's commitments are. Any contract, especially in the textile industry, is likely to have been endorsed by the relevant trade union.

First Days at Work

Your first days at work will seem very strange. For a start, the day will be long and you will feel tired, but you will gradually get used to this. Some jobs may involve working unusual or unsocial hours (this is something you must think about when applying for the job). If you are working in a factory you might find the noise disturbing, but most people get used to it in a short time.

You will change from being one of the oldest and most experienced people at school to being a young and inexperienced employee, and you may not like this! You must expect a certain amount of criticism and advice in your early days, and in turn you must ask questions about anything you are not sure about. Don't struggle on in ignorance and risk making mistakes when a simple question could put you right. Most people are pleased to be asked for their opinions or advice. You will have to take more care over time-keeping and your appearance — if you work with machinery you will as a matter of safety need to keep your hair short or tied back, and leave off jewellery such as bracelets and long necklaces. If you are asked to wear overalls, masks, etc, do so — they are for your own health and safety.

Most firms offer new employees an induction period. Typically, this involves a tour of the factory or firm, to demonstrate how your department fits in with other departments, and to show you the canteen, toilets, and tell you about any sports or social activities organised by the firm. You will also be given training in your job. This may involve working with an experienced member of staff, or it could involve attendance at a college of further education. This is something you should have found out at your interview.

The Manpower Services Commission publishes a booklet called *Workfacts for Young Workers* by Julian Jordan. You can get it from the Careers and Occupational Information Centre (address on page 121).

If You Fail to Get a Job

Try not to feel defeated. It is not you who is at fault. It is easy to say and much harder to do, but try to remain optimistic and interested in life.

If you lounge about all day you will think that life is very boring and pointless, and when you feel like that it is even harder to get a job. Things do change and you should be ready to snatch an opportunity when you see one.

You should continue to look for jobs in the ways suggested earlier in this chapter, and you could take the initiative and write to employers to enquire if they have any vacancies.

Have you thought about doing voluntary work? Besides giving yourself an occupation you will also have the satisfaction of helping other people, or the community. Your local Citizens' Advice Bureau will be able to put you in touch with a project. Community Service Volunteers, 237 Pentonville Road, London N1, recruits volunteers to work full time on projects for a period of between four months and one year. Projects are residential which means that board and lodging are provided and you receive a pocket money allowance of £13 per week (April 1983).

You could think about doing some kind of further education. If you can't find a suitable full-time course, go to part-time day or evening classes and learn some new skill, or follow up a hobby. There is a wide range of courses available, and they are free to those under 19, and the unemployed. Your local library will have details.

Youth Training Scheme

You have probably heard of YOPs, or the Youth Opportunities Programme. This was set up by the Manpower Services Commission on behalf of the government, and in September 1983 was replaced by the Youth Training Scheme. This scheme aims to provide work experience and training for all employed and unemployed 16 year olds who have left full-time education, as well as some unemployed 17 year olds. It will be a year-long programme of planned work experience and work-related training or further education. This 'off the job' training will last for a minimum of 13 weeks. It will give you a broader training than you will receive at work, so you will have a better chance after your year is up of finding work in a range of occupational areas. It should also include some training in what are called 'basic skills': how to communicate with other people (by telephone, letter or in person), how to use numbers, problem solving, and the use of equipment such as computers and the new technologies.

Trainees will be given a training programme at the beginning of the year, and a certificate showing what they have done at the end. The MSC hopes that the scheme will be flexible enough for young people of all abilities to benefit from it. It is also hoped that people with disabilities will be able to fit into the scheme. (If you are disabled, make sure that you contact a specialist careers adviser or Disablement Resettlement Officer, as they will be able to help you. As well as YTS there are other training schemes which are designed specially for the disabled.) While you are on the YTS, you will receive an allowance of £25 per week, plus travel costs over £4 per week. There can be no guarantee of employment at the end of the year, but you will have had a year's work experience and training, which will be valuable assets when you are applying for other jobs.

TOPS Courses

TOPS courses are designed for older people but if

you are 19 or over you can apply. This is the lower age limit, and you must have been out of full-time education for two years and you should not have taken a TOPS course in the last three years. You will be trained in a particular skill or trade, probably at a Skillcentre, and it must be one for which there is a demand, so that the chances of your getting a job after being on a TOPS course are good. At present, areas covered include tailoring, clothing manufacture and machine knitting. Your local Jobcentre or Employment Office will give you more information about TOPS courses.

CHAPTER 9

Salaries

Examples of wages in the textile and clothing industries for the year ending April 1982 are given here, and you should remember that there is usually a percentage increase each year. Most of these rates have been agreed between the appropriate employers' associations and trades unions. Unless otherwise stated they are the basic minimum weekly or hourly rates and do not take into account overtime, bonuses, or other additional payments; 16 and 17 year olds are normally paid a percentage of the adult wage. Full details are given in the Department of Employment publication *Time Rates of Wages and Hours of Work*, issued yearly by Her Majesty's Stationery Office.

Cotton Spinning and Weaving
(Lancashire, Cheshire, Derbyshire, West Yorkshire and Greater Manchester)

Adults 18 years and over — minimum earnings levels (weekly pay)	£
Cotton rooms	
Head	56.73
Assistant Head	56.73

16 year olds get 40 per cent of the adult wage
17 year olds get 50 per cent of the adult wage

Flax and Hemp Preparing, Spinning and Weaving
(Great Britain)

Adults 18 years and over — weekly general minimum time rates	£
Group 1	59.48
Group 2	57.99
Group 3	56.52
Group 4	56.35
Group 5	55.97
Spinners on shifts (nights)	67.62
Weavers during first six months' employment	55.86

Normal weekly hours of work: 40
16 year olds get 40 per cent of the adult wage
17 year olds get 50 per cent of the adult wage

Flax Preparing and Spinning
(Northern Ireland)

Workers 18 years and over — minimum weekly rates
£50.51 (Grade 6) to £63.72 (Grade 1)
Normal weekly hours of work: 40
16 year olds get 70 per cent of the adult wage
17 year olds get 80 per cent of the adult wage

Silk Spinning, Throwing and Weaving

	£
1. Leek	
Grade 1	63.11
Screen printers	65.16
16 year olds	44.69
17 year olds	51.00
2. Macclesfield	
Adults 18 years and over	
Throwing section — time rates	
Grade 1	61.00
Grade 4 (warpers)	62.01
16 year olds	46.69
17 year olds	48.20
Embroidery section	
unskilled	61.00
skilled	61.62

Knitwear Manufacture

1. Scotland except Hawick
   Wages fixed by negotiation within factories.
   Minimum wage £52.50 for a standard week.
2. Hawick
   £36.43 to £41.95 plus £24.10
   non-enhanceable supplement.

Wool Textile Industry

1. Yorkshire — woollen and worsted spinning and weaving	
Adults 18 years and over	£
Group A (including labourers, burlers, knotters and pickers)	60.79
Group B (including weavers — single loom (automatic), weavers — manual, willeyers, mule minders, and all worsted spinning production operatives)	63.74
Group C (including worsted menders, pattern weavers (grade 2))	70.12
Group D (including mule spinners, wool sorters, warp dressers, pattern weavers (grade 1))	76.49
Normal weekly hours of work: 40	
2. West of England	
Adults 18 years and over	
Group D	60.21
to Group A	65.80
3. Yorkshire and East Lancashire — woolcombing and raw wool sector	
Adults 19 years and over — minimum weekly rates	
Overlookers and senior technicians	72.13
16 year olds	37.29
17 year olds	49.37

Narrow Fabrics
Minimum £1.5036 per hour

Made up Textiles
(Great Britain)
Skilled £1.355 per hour
Unskilled £1.295 per hour

Linen and Cotton Handkerchiefs, Household Goods and Linen Piece Goods
1. Great Britain
   Minimum £1.35 per hour
2. Northern Ireland
   Minimum £1.374 to £1.549 per hour
   (after five years' apprenticeship)

Textile Bleaching, Dyeing, Printing and Finishing
1. Lancashire, Derbyshire, West Yorkshire and Greater Manchester
   Minimum weekly rate £63.74
2. Northern Ireland
   Minimum weekly rate £58.81 (Grade 4) to £63.59 (Grade 1)

Hosiery and Knitwear Dyeing and Finishing
(Midlands)
Auxiliary
   Grade 1 £64.00 per week
   Grade 2 £60.00 per week

Clothing Manufacture
1. Corset manufacture
   £1.4263 per hour
2. Dressmaking and women's light clothing
   Cutters with at least three years' experience
   £1.4286 per hour
3. Ready-made and wholesale bespoke tailoring
   Learners of 20 years and over £1.4057 per hour
   After one year's employment £1.4263 per hour
4. Rubber-proofed garment making
   £57.05 per week
5. Shirt collar, tie making, etc
   Trainees, 19 years and over £1.3062 per hour
   Others £1.4263 per hour

6. Wholesale mantle and costume making
   Learners of 20 years and over after
   one year's employment £1.4057 per hour
   Others £1.4263 per hour
7. Hat, cap and millinery
   16 year olds £39.00 per week
   17 year olds £44.07 per week
   19 years and over after one year's
   employment £54.60 per week
   Others £56.55 per week
8. Glove manufacture
   Trainees over 18, unskilled £1.1508 per hour
   Grade 1 £1.3370 per hour

CHAPTER 10

Courses and Useful Addresses

There are several types of college-based course for people who want to learn more about textiles and clothing.

Courses in Textiles and Clothing

First there are general interest or recreational courses, usually held in the evenings, which will add to your knowledge of a subject but will not give you a formal qualification. Some, such as the City and Guilds courses in fashion and embroidery, fall between recreational and vocational. Although they do not give a qualification they can be used as stepping stones to more vocational courses.

There are several short courses providing training in specific work skills. They are administered by the City and Guilds of London Institute (CGLI), the regional examining body for your area, or the college itself.

Other courses teach craft skills and are rather more broadly based. As well as teaching you about the industry in which you work or hope to work, and instructing you in one or more skills, they also aim to add to the general education you had at school, helping you to lead an independent adult life.

Courses leading to awards from the Technician

Education Council (TEC) are intended for technicians. These courses are normally made up of separately assessed units. There are several stages to a TEC programme, and people with different academic qualifications can enter at different stages. They aim to give you a broadly based training so that you will not be restricted to one narrow part of your industry. At the same time you can choose a specialist option to study. There are four main TEC awards: Certificate, Diploma, Higher Certificate and Higher Diploma. The Diploma courses are broader than the Certificate courses and are often, though not always, studied full time.

The minimum entrance requirements for the Certificate/Diploma are usually three CSEs at grade 3, in mathematics, English and a science, but many colleges now prefer grade 1 passes, or O levels. It is sometimes possible to be exempted from part of the course if you have suitable qualifications. Normal progression is from the Certificate/Diploma to the Higher Certificate/Diploma, but with suitable A levels you could go straight into the advanced programme.

The length of the programmes is as follows, assuming that you have the minimum entry qualifications:

Certificate:	three years by day release, possibly less by block release
Diploma:	two years full time, two or three years by sandwich study
Higher Certificate:	two years by day release, possibly less by block release
Higher Diploma:	two years full time, or three years by sandwich study.

Day release means that you are released from your

employment to attend college for one day a week (excluding holidays). Sandwich courses involve periods of study alternating with periods of practical experience in industry. The sandwich may be thin (six months each) or thick (two full years of study, one year in industry, one year of study). Block release is similar except that the periods of study are seldom longer than 12 weeks or one academic term.

Both CGLI and TEC courses have to be approved by the appropriate institutions, but their organisation is the responsibility of the college. Some examples are given here.

City and Guilds 460 — Clothing Craft

This replaces many of the old craft courses in clothing. It offers four specialist options surrounding a 'common core'. The common core teaches you about the industry and clothing production generally, and also helps you to improve your spoken and written communication skills. The options are wholesale cutting, wholesale garment making, retail bespoke cutting, and handcraft tailoring. Each specialism can be studied in three stages with certificates awarded for completion of stages I, II and III. Stages I and II normally take one academic year of one day and one evening per week, and Stage III takes two years.

TEC Certificate in Clothing

There are core units covering garment construction, clothing materials, pattern cutting, garment design, business studies, mathematics and general studies, and you can then do optional units for either further pattern cutting, garment design and sample garment making, or for production organisation and industrial engineering. This course is intended for students working in either the pattern cutting, sample room, or the production department of the light clothing or outerwear sectors.

TEC Higher Certificate in Clothing
This course aims to give students skills and knowledge to prepare them for positions of responsibility at senior supervisory or junior management level. It includes units in pattern cutting, grading, garment design, production organisation, industrial engineering, computer appreciation, marketing, and management of human resources.

TEC Certificate in Textiles (Wool)
This programme consists of 12 units. Six are essential, which are studied by all students, and six are specialist options. Essential units are textile technology, fibre technology, mathematics, physical science (textiles) and communication and general studies. Options can be selected from: textile materials, yarn manufacture, woolcombing, worsted spinning, woollen spinning, woven design, knitted design, fabric manufacture, woven fabrics, knitting technology, textile testing, physical science and mathematics. After completing the course students will be suitable for employment as raw materials sales staff, combing, spinning, weaving, knitting technicians, designers, quality controllers, assistant managers, and work study assistants.

The Higher Certificate goes into these subjects in more depth, and also includes industrial relations, management, and computers. In many colleges you are also given the option of studying for the NEBBS (National Examination Board in Business Studies) Certificate in Supervisory Studies in conjunction with the Higher Certificate.

Courses Available

The following courses were all available during

1982/83 but you should check with your local college to see if they are still being offered. Degree and other courses of high academic standing have not been included. Some short courses which have been established to satisfy local needs have also been omitted.

Abbreviations

BC	Borough College
C	College
CA&T	College of Art and Technology
CD	College of Design
CFE	College of Further Education
CHE	College of Higher Education
CT	College of Technology
CT&D	College of Technology and Design
HE	Higher Education
Inst	Institute
Poly	Polytechnic

TEXTILES

TEC: Certificate in Textile Colouration
Block, Belfast CT
Day Release, Bradford C; Charles Keene CFE, Leicester; Huddersfield TC; Leek CFE; Salford CT; Trent Poly, Nottingham

TEC: Certificate in Textiles
Full Time, Bolton Inst of HE
Block, Belfast CT; Derby Lonsdale CHE
Day Release, Belfast CT; Blackburn CT&D; Bolton Inst of HE; Bradford C; Derby Lonsdale CHE; Hinckley CFE; Huddersfield Poly; Kidderminster CFE; Leek CFE; Oldham CT; Trent Poly, Nottingham

TEC: Certificate in Textiles (Narrow Fabric Manufacture)
Sandwich, Derby Lonsdale CHE

TEC: Certificate in Textiles (Aftercare)
Sandwich, Derby Lonsdale CHE

TEC: Diploma in Textiles
Full Time, Belfast TC; Blackburn CT&D; Bolton Inst of HE; Bradford C; Kidderminster CFE; Trent Poly, Nottingham
Sandwich, Kidderminster CFE

TEC: Higher Certificate in Textile Colouration
Day Release, Bradford C; Leicester Poly; Manchester Poly; Salford CT; Trent Poly, Nottingham
Evening, Leicester Poly

TEC: Higher Certificate in Textiles
Full Time, Bolton Inst of HE
Day Release, Belfast CT; Blackburn CT&D; Bolton Inst of HE; Bradford C; Derby Lonsdale CHE; Huddersfield Poly; Leicester Poly; Oldham CT; Trent Poly, Nottingham
Evening, Leicester Poly

TEC: Higher Certificate in Textiles (Narrow Fabric Manufacture)
Sandwich, Derby Lonsdale CHE

TEC: Higher Certificate in Textiles (Aftercare)
Sandwich, Derby Lonsdale CHE

TEC: Higher Diploma in Textile Colouration
Full Time, Leicester Poly
Day Release, Salford CT

TEC: Higher Diploma in Textiles
Full Time, Bolton Inst of HE; Bradford C; Leicester Poly; Trent Poly, Nottingham

TEC: Higher Diploma in Textiles
Full Time, Bolton Inst of HE; Bradford C; Leicester Poly; Trent Poly, Nottingham

SCOTEC: Certificate in the Dyeing of Textiles
Block, Scottish C Textiles, Galashiels
Day Release, Reid Kerr C, Paisley

SCOTEC: Certificate in Textiles
Block, Scottish C Textiles,Galashiels
Day Release, Dundee CT; Henderson TC, Hawick; Moray CFE, Elgin

SCOTEC: Higher Certificate in the Dyeing of Textiles
Block, Scottish C Textiles, Galashiels
Day Release, Reid Kerr C, Paisley

SCOTEC: Higher Certificate in Textiles
Block, Scottish C Textiles, Galashiels
Day Release, Henderson TC, Hawick
Evening, Henderson TC, Hawick

National Examinations Board for Supervisory Studies: Certificate in Supervisory Studies (Textile Industry)
Block, Stoke Cauldon CFE
Day Release, West Nottinghamshire CFE, Mansfield; Stoke Cauldon CFE
Evening, Stoke Cauldon CFE

Training Services Division: TOPS Harris Tweed Weaver Training Course
Full Time, Lews Castle C, Stornoway

CGLI 414: Textile Techniques, stage I
Full Time, Kidderminster CFE
Block, Belfast CT; Burnley CA&T
Day Release, Blackburn CT&D; Bolton Inst of HE; Bradford C; Braintree CFE; Burnley CA&T; Mid-Gloucestershire TC, Stroud; Oldham CT; Derbyshire C, Ilkeston
Evening, Bolton Inst of HE; Oldham CT

CGLI 414: Textile Techniques, stage II
Full Time, Kidderminster CFE
Block, Burnley CA&T
Day Release, Blackburn CT&D; Bolton Inst of HE; Bradford C; Burnley CA&T; Mid-Gloucestershire TC, Stroud; Oldham CT
Evening, Bolton Inst of HE; Oldham CT

CGLI 414: Textile Techniques, stage III
Block, Burnley CA&T
Day Release, Blackburn CT&D; Bolton Inst of HE; Bradford C; Burnley CA&T; Mid-Gloucestershire TC, Stroud; Oldham CT
Evening, Bolton Inst of HE; Oldham CT

CGLI 427 Cotton and Allied Textile Technicians: Final, Weaving (Cotton and Man-Made Fibres)
Day Release, Blackburn CT&D; Bolton Inst of HE

CGLI 427 Cotton and Allied Textile Technicians: Final, Yarn Production (Short Staple System)
Day Release, Blackburn CT&D; Bolton Inst of HE; Oldham CT

Regional Award: 425 Foundation Course in Textiles
Day Release, Oldham CT

Regional Award: West of England (Certificate in Textiles)
Day Release, Mid-Gloucestershire TC, Stroud

College Award: Certificate in Dyeing of Textiles
Block, Scottish C Textiles, Galashiels

College Award: Certificate in Textile and Knitting Technology
Full Time, Leicester Poly

College Award: Certificate in Textile Merchandising
Full Time, C for Distributive Trades, London

College Award: Certificate in Textiles
Day Release, C for Distributive Trades, London
Evening, C for Distributive Trades, London

College Award: Certificate in Textile Technology
Full Time, Lews Castle C, Stornoway

College Award: Diploma in Carpet Technology
Full Time, Kidderminster, CFE
Sandwich, Kidderminster CFE

College Award: Diploma in Textiles
Full Time, Dundee CT

College Award: Diploma in Textile Technology
Full Time, Bradford C; Scottish C Textiles, Galashiels

College Award: Diploma in Textile and Knitwear Technology
Full Time, Leicester Poly

College Based: Cotton Fibre Technology, Testing and Evaluation
Block, Bolton Inst of HE

College Based: Non-Woven Textiles
Evening, Bolton Inst of HE

College Based: Sizing of Spun Yarn
Block, Bolton Inst of HE

CLOTHING AND TAILORING

TEC: Certificate in Clothing
Full Time, Handsworth TC; Kilburn Poly, London; Oxford CFE; Southgate TC, London
Day Release, Belfast CT; Handsworth TC; Jacob Kramer C, Leeds; London C Fashion; Mabel Fletcher TC, Liverpool; Manchester Poly; Southgate TC, London
Evening, London C Fashion

TEC: Diploma in Clothing
Full Time, Belfast CT; Handsworth TC; Jacob Kramer C, Leeds; London C Fashion; Manchester Poly; Medway CD, Rochester; Oxford CFE; Southgate TC, London
Day Release, Handsworth TC

TEC: Higher Certificate in Clothing
Day Release, Belfast CT; London C Fashion
Evening, London C Fashion

TEC: Higher Diploma in Clothing
Full Time, London C Fashion; Manchester Poly; Medway CD, Rochester

SCOTEC: Certificate in Clothing
Day Release, Barmulloch C, Glasgow; Cardonald C, Glasgow

SCOTEC: Certificate in Knitting Techniques
Full Time, Lerwick FEC

SCOTEC: Higher Certificate in Clothing
Full Time, Cardonald C, Glasgow
Day Release, Cardonald C, Glasgow

Training Services Division: TOPS Course in Clothing Production
Full Time, Cardonald C, Glasgow

Training Services Division: TOPS Course for Clothing Technicians
Full Time, Cardonald C, Glasgow
Second Chance, Cardonald C, Glasgow

Training Services Division: TOPS Course in Fashion and Garment Manufacture
Full Time, Mid-Warwickshire CFE, Leamington Spa

Training Services Division: TOPS Course in Machine Knitting
Full Time, Lerwick FEC; Lews Castle C, Stornoway

Training Services Division: TOPS Course for Sewing Machinists
Full Time, Cardonald C, Glasgow; Rockingham CFE
Second Chance, Cardonald C, Glasgow

The following colleges also offer CGLI courses in clothing. Details have not been given because many of the courses are in the process of being replaced by the new course 460 — Clothing Craft.

Barnfield C, Luton; Belfast CT; Bishop Auckland TC; Cannock Chase TC; Cardonald C, Glasgow; Chesterfield CA&D; Clarendon CFE, Nottingham; Cleveland TC; Colchester Inst; Cricklade C, Andover; Crosskeys CFE; Dacorum C, Hemel Hempstead; Doncaster IHE; Dudley CT; Erith CT; Fermanagh CFE; Gateshead TC; Handsworth TC; Hounslow BC; Isle of Ely C; Jacob Kramer C, Leeds; Leek CFE; Limavady TC; London C Fashion; Mabel Fletcher TC, Liverpool; North East Wales IHE, Wrexham; Oldham CT; Oxford CFE; Plymouth CA&D; Redbridge TC; Shipley C; Shrewsbury CAT; Somerset CA&T, Taunton; South Cheshire CFE, Crewe; SE Derbyshire C, Ilkeston; Southgate TC, London; Southampton CHE; Stoke Cauldon CFE; Tameside CT, Ashton under Lyne; Tresham C, Kettering and Corby; Waltham Forest C; Wigan CT; York CA&T

Regional Award: 789 Home Machine Knitting
Day Release, Cardonald C, Glasgow
Evening, Mabel Fletcher TC, Liverpool

College awards are offered by the following colleges (full time unless otherwise stated):

London C Fashion (Cert in Clothing Technology; Cert in Bespoke Tailoring; Cert in Theatrical Costume and Cutting; Cert in Wholesale Tailoring; Dip in Clothing Production; Dip in Tailoring).
Mabel Fletcher C, Liverpool, (Cert in Clothing Technology — block; Sewing Machinist Instructor's Cert — block and day release; Cert for Supervisors in the Clothing Industry — block; Dip in Clothing Manufacture and Retail Fashion; Dip in Tailoring).
Cardonald C, Glasgow, (Junior Technician's Cert in Garment and Fashion Technology)
Lerwick FEC (Course in Fair Isle Hand Knitting — day release and second chance).

FASHION AND TEXTILE DESIGN

DATEC: Certificate in Design for Clothing Manufacture
Full Time, Somerset CA&T, Taunton

DATEC: Certificate in Fashion
Full Time, Bournville SA&C; Granville C, Sheffield; Tameside CT, Ashton under Lyne; Waltham Forest C; Wigan CT
Day Release, Scarborough TC; Southampton CHE

DATEC: Certificate in Fashion (Light Clothing)
Full Time, Cleveland CA&D, Middlesbrough

DATEC: Diploma in Fashion
Full Time, Barnfield C, Luton; Berkshire CA&D, Maidenhead; Bournemouth & Poole CA&D; Bradford C; Croydon C; Derby Lonsdale CHE; Doncaster IHE; Epsom SA&D; Granville C, Sheffield; Hounslow BC; Jacob Kramer C, Leeds; London C Fashion; Loughborough CA&D; Medway CD, Rochester; Newcastle CA&D; Plymouth CA&D; Salisbury CA; Southampton CHE; Southend CT; Stafford CFE; Stoke Cauldon CFE; West Nottinghamshire CFE, Mansfield; West Sussex CD, Chichester; Wigan CT; York CA&T
Day Release, Gloucestershire CAT, Gloucester

DATEC: Diploma in Surface Pattern Design
Full Time, Jacob Kramer C, Leeds

DATEC: Diploma in Textile Design
Full Time, Bradford C; Derby Lonsdale CHE; West Sussex CD, Chichester

DATEC: Diploma in Fashion and Textiles
Full Time, Bradford C; Canterbury CA

DATEC: Higher Certificate in Fashion
Full Time, Stafford CFE

DATEC: Higher Diploma in Fashion
Full Time, Bournemouth & Poole CA&D; Derby Lonsdale CHE; London C Fashion; Medway CD, Rochester
Day Release, Cleveland CA&D, Middlesbrough

DATEC: Higher Diploma in Textile Design
Full Time, Derby Lonsdale CHE
Day Release, Cleveland CA&D, Middlesbrough

Regional Award: Certificate in Fashion and Clothing Design
Day Release, Bishop Auckland TC
Evening, Bishop Auckland TC

Regional Award: Certificate in Fashion Design
Full Time, Dewsbury and Batley T&AC; York CA&T

Regional Award: Post-Certificate in Fashion Design
Full Time, Granville C, Sheffield

Regional Award: Certificate in Fashion and Textiles
Full Time, Scarborough TC

Regional Award: Certificate in Surface Pattern Design
Full Time, Barnsley CAD

Regional Award: Certificate in Textile Design
Full Time, Dewsbury and Batley T&AC

Regional Award: 758 Manufacturing and Retail Fashion (Certificate in Art and Design)
Full Time, Burnley CA&T; Oldham CT; Southport CAD

Regional Award: 758 Textile and Pattern Design (Certificate in Art and Design)
Full Time, Blackburn CT&D; Rochdale CA; Southport CAD; Stockport CT
Day Release, Walsall CA

Regional Award: Diploma in Applied Design (Textile/Fashion)
Full Time, Monkwearmouth CFE

Regional Award: Diploma in Art and Design (Fashion)
Full Time, Chelsea SA, London

Regional Award: Diploma in Art and Design (Textile Design)
Full Time, Chelsea SA, London; West Surrey CA&D, Farnham

Regional Award: Higher Diploma in Art and Design (Textile Design)
Full Time, Reigate SA&D
Day Release, Cleveland CA&D, Middlesbrough

Regional Award: Diploma in Design (Fashion)
Full Time, Salisbury CA, Somerset CA&T

Regional Award: Higher Diploma in Design (Fashion)
Full Time, Berkshire CA&D
Day Release, Cleveland CA&D, Middlesbrough

Regional Award: Diploma in Design (Textile Design)
Full Time, Southend CT

Regional Award: Diploma in Fashion
Full Time, Plymouth CA&D; Southampton CHE

Regional Award: Higher Diploma in Fashion Design
Full Time, Epsom SA&D

Regional Award: Diploma in Textile and Surface Pattern Design
Full Time, Somerset CA&T, Taunton

College Award: Design Technician Certificate (Fashion)
Full Time, Bournville SA&C

College Award: Certificate in Dress and Light Clothing
Full Time, London C Fashion

College Award: Certificate in Fashion
Full Time, Merton TC, London; Nene C, Northampton

College Award: Certificate in Fashion Design
Full Time, Eastbourne CFE

College Award: Certificate in Textile Arts and Fashion
Day Release, Sheffield City Poly
Evening, Sheffield City Poly

College Award: Certificate in Textile and Knitwear Design
Full Time, South Fields CFE, Leicester

College Award: Certificate in Textiles (Printed)
Full Time, Eastbourne CFE

College Award: Certificate in Textiles (Woven) including Rugs and Carpets
Full Time, Eastbourne CFE

College Award: Advanced Certificate in Fashion Design
Full Time, Salford CT

College Award: Pre-CGLI Certificate in Fashion
Evening, South Gwent CFE

College Award, Diploma in Carpet Design
Sandwich, Kidderminster CFE

College Award: Diploma in Dress and Fashion
Full-time, Mid-Warwickshire CFE, Leamington Spa

College Award: Diploma in Dress and Light Clothing
Full Time, London C Fashion; Redbridge TC

College Award: Diploma in Fashion
Full Time, Amersham CFEA&D; Coventry TC; East Warwickshire CFE, Rugby; Gwent CHE, Newport; Stafford CFE; Ulster Poly; Weston super Mare TC&SA

College Award: Diploma in Fashion Design
Full Time, Bolton TC; Chesterfield CA&D; Derby Lonsdale CHE; Dyfed CA, Carmarthen; London C Fashion; North East Wales IHE, Wrexham

College Award: Diploma in Fashion Technology
Day Release, Gloucestershire CAT, Gloucester

College Award: Diploma in Fashion, Textiles and Marketing
Full Time, Hastings CAT

College Award: Diploma in Printed and Woven Textiles
Full Time, Huddersfield Poly

College Award: Advanced Diploma in Printed Textiles
Full Time, West Sussex CD, Chichester

College Award: Diploma in Surface Pattern and Textile Construction
Full Time, Bolton TC

College Award: Diploma in Textile Design
Full Time, Amersham CFEA&D; Blackburn CT&D; Croydon C; Derby Lonsdale CHE; North East Wales IHE, Wrexham

College Award: Diploma in Textiles and Printed Surfaces
Full Time, Dewsbury and Batley T&AC

College Award: Diploma in Woven Textiles
Full Time, Bolton TC

College Award: Diploma in Woven Textile Design
Full Time, Dyfed CA, Carmarthen

College Award: Advanced Diploma in Fashion Design
Full Time, West Sussex CD, Chichester

College Based: Advanced Diploma in Fashion Design
Full Time, Barnet C; Salford CT

Useful Addresses

Association of Scientific, Technical and Managerial Staffs
East Road, Longsight, Manchester M12 5GY

British Man-Made Fibres Federation
24 Buckingham Gate, London SW1E 6LB

British Textile Employers' Association
Room 272, 2nd Floor, Royal Exchange, Manchester M2 7ED

British Wool Marketing Board
Oak Mills, Station Road, Clayton, Bradford, West Yorkshire BD4 6JD

Careers and Occupational Information Centre
Department CW, Moorfoot, Sheffield S1 4PQ

City and Guilds of London Institute
76 Portland Place, London W1N 4AA

Clothing and Allied Products Industry Training Board
Tower House, Merrion Way, Leeds, West Yorkshire
LS2 8NY

Clothing and Footwear Institute
Albert Road, Hendon, London NW4

Confederation of British Wool Textiles Limited
60 Toller Lane, Bradford, West Yorkshire BD8 9DA

Council for National Academic Awards
344-5 Gray's Inn Road, London WC1X 8BP

Dyers, Bleachers and Textile Workers National Trade Group
National House, Sunbridge Road, Bradford, West Yorkshire
BD1 2QB

ICI Fibres
Hookstone Road, Harrogate, North Yorkshire HG2 8QN

International Institute for Cotton
Kingston Road, Didsbury, Manchester M20 8RD

Irish Linen Guild
Morley House, 70-71 New Bond Street, London W1Y 9DE

Man-Made Fibres Training Advisory Board
Langwood House, 63-81 High Street, Rickmansworth,
Hertfordshire WD3 1EQ

SCOTEC (Scottish Technician Education Council)
38 Queen Street, Glasgow G1 3DY

Shirley Institute
Didsbury, Manchester M20 8RX

Silk Association
c/o Rheinbergs Ltd, Sovereign Way, Tonbridge, Kent
TN9 1RN

Silk Educational Services
37 Chinbrook Road, Grove Park, London SE12

Society of Dyers and Colourists
Perkin House, PO Box 244, 82 Grattan Road, Bradford,
West Yorkshire BD1 2JB

TEC (Technician Education Council)
Central House, Upper Woburn Place, London WC1H 0HH

The Textile Institute
10 Blackfriars Street, Manchester M3 5DR

Books to Read

Ball, Linda, *Careers in Art and Design* (second edition), Kogan Page, 1983

Brearley, Alan and Iredale, John, *The Woollen Industry* (second edition), Leeds, Wira, 1977

Careers and Occupational Information Centre (booklets), 'First steps in thinking about jobs and careers', by C and M Ball; 'Workfacts for young workers', by J Jordan; 'Working in the clothing industry', by E Hoult

CRAC, *Directory of Further Education*, Cambridge, Hobsons Press Ltd, 1982

Gale, Elizabeth, *From Fibres to Fabrics* (third edition), Mills & Boon, 1978

Humphrey, Paul, *Textiles*, Hove, Wayland, 1982

Kurth, Heinz, *Textiles*, World's Work, 1977

Messenger, B, *Picking up the Linen Threads*, University of Texas Press, 1978

Miles, Lewis, *Cotton*, Hove, Wayland, 1980

Thomson, Helen, *Fibres and Fabrics of Today*, Heinemann, 1972

Watson, Tom and Jenny, *Wool*, Hove, Wayland, 1980

CHAPTER 11

Glossary

Bale A large sack or bag in which raw material is compressed and packed.

Band knife A large electric cutter, used for cutting a lay of cloth.

Blending The mixing of fibres of different origins, qualities, colours, etc, in preparation for carding and spinning.

Bobbin A tube on which yarn or roving is wound.

Boll The cotton seed pod.

Burling and mending The removal of minor defects in a finished cloth.

Carding The process of untangling and straightening out natural fibres.

Cellulose The material of which the cell walls in plants and trees are made.

Combing The process carried out before spinning high quality cotton and worsted yarns to remove short fibres, leaving long, parallel fibres.

Cone A conical package of yarn.

Crimp The waviness in a fibre.

Drawing or **Drafting** The process of blending fibres into a sliver which is then drawn into a finer roving ready for spinning.

Extrusion The forcing of a chemical liquid through spinnerets to produce man-made fibre filaments.

Fibre A strand of textile material.

Filament A continuous thread of silk or a man-made fibre.

Flax The plant from which linen is made.

Fleece The coat of the sheep which is shorn off in one piece.

Folding The twisting together of single yarns to give strength or a special effect; the result is a folded or plied yarn.

Ginning The process of separating cotton fibres from seed.
Goose A hand-held iron used in bespoke tailoring.

Hackling The process of removing dirt from and straightening out flax fibres.
Heald A cord or wire with an eyelet through which a warp yarn is threaded.

Lay Layers of cloth ready for cutting in wholesale clothing manufacture.
Line Long fibres of flax.
Loom A machine on which fabrics are woven.

Marker A piece of paper, the same width as the cloth, from which a pattern for a garment is to be cut.
Mercerising A process in which fabrics are soaked in caustic soda and then stretched to make them more lustrous and receptive to dyes.

Noils Short wool fibres which are removed during combing. They can be used to make felt.

Perching The inspection of woven fabric for faults.
Picking The passage of the weft thread through the shed.
Piece A roll of cloth.

Reed An instrument similar in appearance to a heavy comb, through which warp ends are drawn.
Retting The process of soaking flax in water to free the fibres.
Rippling The process of removing the seeds from the flax plant.
Roving A relatively fine yarn ready for spinning.

Scutching The beating and drying of raw flax to separate the fibres.
Shearing The process of cutting the wool from the sheep.
Shedding The parting of warp threads in weaving to allow the weft to pass through.
Sliver A loose rope of carded fibres.
Slubbing A rope of twisted fibre about 7mm thick.
Spindle A tapered peg, rotated to insert twist in the yarn during spinning.
Spinneret The part of a silkworm which spins the silk filament. Also the device which is used to form man-made fibre filaments.

Spinning The process of turning roving into yarn by drawing and twisting.
Staple Length The average length of natural fibre, cut silk, or man-made filaments.

Toile A sample garment made in a cheap fabric which serves as a pattern.
Tops Long fibres used in worsted manufacture.
Tow Short fibres of flax.
Twisting see *Folding*.

Warp The lengthwise threads in a woven piece of cloth.
Warping The placing of warp threads side by side on a beam ready for weaving.
Weaving The process by which a yarn is threaded over and under other yarns which cross the first ones at right angles to make cloth.
Weft The crosswise threads in a woven piece of cloth.
Winding The transferring of yarns on to suitable packages for weaving or knitting.

Yarn A continuous strand of twisted fibres formed by spinning. Used in weaving and knitting.